THE FAMILY DOG
Its Choice and Training

The author with some of his dogs
(*Sally Anne Thompson*)

THE
FAMILY DOG
Its Choice and Training

A Practical Guide for Every Dog Owner

JOHN HOLMES

ARCO PUBLISHING COMPANY INC.
NEW YORK

Published in the United States by
ARCO PUBLISHING COMPANY, INC.
219 Park Avenue South, New York, N.Y. 10003

First published (as *The Choice and Training of
the Family Dog*) 1957
Second edition 1958
Third edition 1962
Fourth edition 1966
Fifth edition (as *The Family Dog*) 1970
Sixth edition 1972
Seventh edition 1975
Revised editions © John Holmes 1958, 1962, 1970, and 1975

Library of Congress Catalog Card Number : 75–29967
ISBN : 0 668–03927–2

Printed in Great Britain

To all the good dogs I have known, especially the difficult ones, who taught me as much as I taught them, but who, in the end, became willing servants and staunch friends

CONTENTS

7

ILLUSTRATIONS

*The photographs taken by Howard Evans and
Sally Anne Thompson are of the author's own dogs*

9

AUTHOR'S INTRODUCTION

How time flies! It is now over ten years since this book was first published. Years which have made history in many and diverse spheres. Years which have been remarkable for an ever-increasing thirst for knowledge. Never in the history of mankind have so many books been published on so many different subjects. And dogs come high in the list.

There has also been an increase in the scientific study of animal behaviour and an even greater increase in the information made available to the general public. Scientists have written of their experiments in language which can be understood by the layman and this information has been illustrated on several occasions in serious television programmes.

One would expect all this to create a better understanding between man and dog. And because of this understanding one could expect a marked reduction in the number of dog problems throughout the country. But there is no evidence to suggest that this is so. The introduction to the first edition of this book started:

Every year in Great Britain some 10,000 sheep and poultry are torn to pieces by dogs; one in every seven road accidents is caused by dogs, involving some 75,000 canine and 3,000 human casualties; people are bitten by dogs (often their own); streets are fouled by dogs; thousands of homes are ruled, often ruined, by dogs. For such a state of affairs to exist shows there is something wrong. For it to exist in a country which boasts of being a nation of dog lovers, where the dog is held in higher esteem than anywhere else in the world, shows there is something very wrong indeed.

Unfortunately all that applies just as much today as it did in 1957. Indeed the Ministry of Agriculture figures show that in England and Wales 9,070 sheep were killed or injured by dogs in 1966 compared with 5,626 in 1956. So there is indeed something very far wrong and I believe that the following remarks which I made in my first introduction are as true as they were then.

There are many reasons for the appalling amount of dog trouble in this country, but I am convinced that the fundamental cause of it all lies in the fact that very few dog-owners know what a dog is. They buy 'just as a pet' an animal which was never intended, and in many cases is quite unsuitable, for the part. They believe they are looking after it well if they feed and house it properly. Many would do better to keep a budgerigar or a tortoise, being oblivious to the fact that, to this animal with its highly developed brain, mental well-being is more important than physical. Few give sufficient consideration to the responsibility they are taking upon themselves when they acquire a dog. There must be many who, if they realized how great that responsibility is, would decide not to keep a dog at all. If more people made such a decision there would be fewer unhappy dogs, fewer disappointed owners and a great deal less trouble all round.

It is indeed unfortunate that the dog which has served and still serves man so well in so many ways for so many years should now all too often prove to be anything from a nuisance to a menace. Even more unfortunate is the fact that this state of affairs is gradually becoming worse.

There are several reasons for this, the most obvious probably being that so few people seem to realize that it exists. Fewer still have any practical suggestions as to how it can be solved. Every now and then the N.F.U. sets up a great hue and cry about stray dogs, but the suggestions put forward to solve the problem prove a complete inability to understand it. In many cases their stupidity makes me quite ashamed of my farming connections.

Some think that training classes to help owners to train their dogs should solve the problem. I am all in favour of well-run training classes but, while the number of these has increased enormously in recent years, there has been no decrease at all in the number of problem dogs. It is significant that, of the owners who ask me for advice, at least half have been attending training classes for some time. So training classes are obviously not the answer either—and neither is training in itself.

To find the answer to any problem the first task should be to find the cause. In this case there are two major causes. As I already said, the fundamental one arises from the fact that so few owners know what a dog is—and many don't even want to find out. So long as it shows some signs of affection and, more important, allows its owner to smother it with 'love' they are quite happy. Whether or not the dog is happy matters not the slightest.

It is this aspect of dog ownership which at times makes my task as a writer so frustrating. In this book I tried to help my reader to understand his or her own dog and I was delighted when this was mentioned in several of the press reviews. But I get letters from readers who start by saying 'I have read your book and found it very interesting but . . .' and they then proceed to tell me in great detail of the difficulty they are having with their dog. As I read on I realize more and more that if they have read the book they obviously have not understood it—a very depressing thought for any writer! On investigation, however, I often find that they have not in fact read the book at all. If their dog pulls on the lead they turn up the chapter on learning to walk on the lead; if it fights they look up 'fighting'. But they won't start at the beginning and read the book right through in an effort to find out what a dog is and how its mind works.

The importance of this cannot be over emphasized. Most of my knowledge I have gained from the study of dogs, not of books. One can learn more about control by watching a pack leader control his pack or about correction and reward by watching a bitch with her puppies than one can learn from any book. But few dog owners have such opportunities. That is why I try in this book to impart some of the knowledge I have gained in this way.

In doing so I shall no doubt disillusion many people who like to believe that their dog is 'almost human' and that it 'understands every word I say to him'. But, if they are disappointed to learn of the things that dogs cannot do, I hope this will be offset by more knowledge of what they can do. Few owners appreciate the capabilities of their own dog. Only a minority of owners have any idea of the pleasure and companionship to be derived from a dog, sensibly brought up *as a dog*. Here I might mention that, although, throughout the book, I use the familiar term 'pet dog', at no time have I in mind those poor creatures kept solely as outlets for the depraved affection of their owners. A dog, of course, can be a pet as well as a companion, guard and servant. Those who desire to degrade it to the status of *just a pet*, however, are unlikely to agree with what I have to say.

The second reason for the prevalence of problem dogs and dog problems is the scarcity of trainable dogs. While the number of dogs keeps increasing the number of dogs temperamentally suited to living under present day conditions continues to decrease.

Although the reason for this is obvious the solution is not so easy to find. In days of old dogs were kept for a purpose—to work sheep, to hunt, guard and for many other practical uses. Those which were good at the job were bred from; those which were not were shot! The result of this crude but effective system of selective breeding was a high percentage of good dogs—sane dogs with character and intelligence.

But we have become more civilized now. We don't shoot a dog just because he is a nut case! Provided he conforms to the Kennel Club standard of points for his particular breed, we breed from him. And produce more nut cases, some of which may be even closer to physical perfection. Those which are not will be sold as pets to the unsuspecting public. It is now some twenty years since I wrote an article in the canine press accusing dog breeders of using the pet market as a dustbin into which they threw their rubbish. This was not very popular at the time but I am afraid I shall have to remain unpopular by saying that the same still applies.

At that time puppies bred in show kennels but not up to show standard were the chief source of supply of family dogs. But, as a result of the great boom in animal sanctuaries, another supply of pet dogs has now become available. These sanctuaries—what a high-sounding word—provide an outlet for the sentimentality of many well meaning animal lovers. They provide an outlet for the selfishness of many people who have to part with a dog. Those who cannot be bothered to find a suitable home and have not the courage to have it put to sleep. It is so much easier to say to the family and neighbours 'He has gone to a sanctuary' than 'I had him put down'.

So far as the dog is concerned he has merely gone to gaol—possibly for life. Some of these sanctuaries can be compared to the very worst type of concentration camp—others to our most modern prisons. But they are all prisons. As with all prisoners, some dogs accept the conditions and lead reasonably happy lives. These, however, form the minority. The majority of dogs in sanctuaries are there because someone did not want them at home. They are delinquents, vagrants and others quite unsuited as pets in a modern society. And it is very cruel to keep them confined for years as often happens. It is not usually intended to keep them for life and efforts are made to find 'good homes' for these dogs. It is because my postbag reveals an ever-increasing number of problem dogs originating from sanctuaries that I feel I must warn readers to be very careful before accepting one. Some marvellous dogs do come from sanctuaries of one sort or another (we have had some ourselves) but that does not alter the fact that many will never settle as pets. Sorry as I feel for them, the only possible way one could do them a good turn would be to offer them a home and then have them put down.

For some inexplicable reason animal lovers who relish their beef, mutton, pork or chicken are horrified at the idea of putting a dog to sleep. The result is that this country is overrun with dogs. And while their overall numbers increase the number temperamentally suited to live as pets under present-day conditions continues to decrease.

I had no early ambitions as an author and dog trainer—farming being the career I chose. This was not surprising, as my pedigree showed that I was bred for nothing else. My chief interests lay in animals, not any particular breed or species, but just animals, wild or domestic.

From the age of eleven I had a Shetland pony which I drove like mad in a trap, and when young horses had to be broken I was usually the sole assistant. This taught me not only to do what I was told, but to do it quickly and to keep my wits about me without getting into a panic. When, due to my own carelessness, my pony ran away and got killed by a car (I cried for days), it was to be a lifelong reminder to me of the responsibility of owning an animal.

There were, of course, always people to talk to about animals, mostly dogs. Shepherds, drovers, gamekeepers, poachers and others, such as 'Old Moley' the mole- and rat-catcher (a 'Pests Officer' nowadays), whose ferrets answered their names just like dogs. These men were no intellectuals, they had made no scientific study of animals, but they were *real* men who kept *real* dogs which worked and enjoyed working *with* a master rather than *for* one.

When I finished my education at an agricultural college, it was not surprising that the job I should want was that of shepherd and cattleman, one of the few jobs left where one has time to think and to study the animals in one's care. I then came in contact with more dogs and more shepherds who worked dogs. Being keen on dogs in general, I started breeding and exhibiting Welsh Corgis as a hobby, with some remarkable 'beginner's luck'.

During World War II I came south of the Border, and after the war, when classes started up again, took a great interest in obedience training. Here I met many famous trainers with a much more scientific approach to the subject than those to whom I have been referring. On putting their advice into practice, however, I came to the conclusion that their principles were the same, although often easier to understand. After some success in obedience competitions, I decided to 'turn professional' by taking dogs belonging to other people for training. My wife and I also built up a team of demonstration dogs with which we gave displays all over the British Isles. Following this we started training dogs for the film and television business.

All this has brought me in contact, directly or indirectly, with thousands of dog owners of a very different type from those referred to above. These are the people who keep a dog 'just as a pet' or as a companion and guard. They come from every walk in life, they form by far the largest number of dog owners in this country—and their dogs cause the greatest amount of trouble. Few have the slightest idea what a dog really is and, at first, I felt inclined to regard them all as damn fools. On getting to know them better, however, and in trying to see things from their point of view, I came to realize that much of this ignorance is due, not so much to lack of desire to learn as to lack of opportunity. When I compare my own up-bringing with that of dog owners, brought up in a town in a mechanical age, I realize how difficult it must be for them to understand things which to me have always seemed obvious. My first purpose in writing this book is to try to impart to those people some dog sense; which I regard as an understanding of the canine mind which enables one to see things from the dogs' point of view.

As the most important factor in having a well-trained dog lies in having the right dog to train, I have devoted as much space to explaining what a dog is and how to find the right one as to training. Far too little attention is usually paid to the choice of a dog and I hear many sad tales of dogs that have gone wrong (the owner usually wondering what mistakes he or she has made) owing to their unsuitability to the conditions under which they were kept. In many cases the owners have been 'sold a pup' at a good price by well-known breeders who knew, or should have known, that the chances of it being a success were practically non-existent. Some of what I say is likely to be unpopular with many dog breeders, who are far too ready to blame the 'stupid owner' for the faults which they have bred into the puppies they sell. My object, however, is not to boost the sale of dogs, but to help to avoid disappoint-ment to those who buy them.

To be able to train dogs to a high standard, especially to train *any* dog to a high standard, is not only a gift, it requires skill acquired only through practice. Only a minority of dog owners, however, have any desire to train their dogs to a high standard. All they want is a well-behaved member of the family. While admitting that there are people who cannot train a dog, just as there are people who cannot dance or skate, no matter how much they try, I am convinced that, without experience and without being gifted in this direction, nearly all owners could train a *trainable* dog—if they make up their minds to it.

In spite of the dog's widespread popularity, few owners, I find, have any idea of the real value of a well-trained dog. Many stories am I told, in all good faith, of 'almost human'

B

accomplishments which are purely imaginary. If any of my dogs resembled, in any way, some of the people I know I should have them destroyed immediately! The title of 'man's best friend' was won by the dog's ability to do so many things which no human being could attempt and which few people realize are possible. If, therefore, I create a certain amount of disillusionment by pointing out what dogs cannot do, I hope to more than make up for it by helping readers to appreciate what they *can* do.

Last, but by no means least, is the pleasure or unhappiness of the dogs themselves. Much publicity is rightly given to wanton cruelty; also to alleged cruelty in training. You can decide for yourself whether the methods described are cruel, but the unhappiest dogs I meet are untrained. In my opinion, by far the greatest amount of suffering to dogs in this country is caused by people whose only intentions are to be kind; but who, through lack of dog sense, cause great mental suffering to the dogs they love so much.

The methods of training I describe have been gleaned from many sources and, necessity being the mother of invention, several have been invented by myself. Although they are the most effective methods I know at the time of writing, it does not follow that they are the only methods, or that it is impossible to improve on them. Opinions differ in nothing more than the training of dogs.

As I have said, some people are unable to train a dog no matter how hard they try, but I should like to emphasize that no book on training should be taken too literally. Training a dog, especially a clever dog, is a battle of wits. No one goes to a debate armed only with a book. They go armed with a knowledge of their subject (perhaps acquired through reading books) which they use, or hope to use, in conjunction with their alertness of mind to 'overpower' their opponent. It seems to me that those who benefited and are likely to benefit most from this book are those who read it as a whole and use the knowledge so gained to help them to anticipate the problems that are likely to crop up rather than waiting until a problem is already there.

My objects in writing are, firstly, to help you to find a dog you can train and, secondly, to help you to train it with as little trouble as possible. Not to train it for any specialized job but simply to help it to grow into a happy, sensible servant and friend of the family; the sort of dog so many want and so few seem to find.

1970 **J. H.**

Six photographs have been replaced in this seventh edition, but I have not found it necessary to make any major amendments to the text.

1975 J. H.

PART I

THEORY

CHAPTER I

HUNTING AND PACK INSTINCTS

In the wild dog—In the domestic dog

LET us first consider what a dog is; what the mental ingredients are which enabled this animal so deservedly to win the title of 'man's best friend'. Before doing this, however, we must consider what a dog *was*.

Even experts' opinions differ as to its origin, but there seems little doubt that, despite the tremendous variation in type, all domestic dogs are descended from a mixture of species, many of which are still to be found in a wild state. These are the wolves, jackals, foxes, etc., which collectively form one of the meanest, most cowardly and cunning groups of animals.

Among wild dogs were some that lived in packs, some alone. The majority were hunters, but a few were scavengers which lived on the leavings of these hunters and by scrounging around the dwelling-places of man. In spite of many that were undesirable, some wild dogs had characteristics which could be useful to mankind. Although, in all animals, wild or tame, each breed or species has certain common characteristics, the strength of these varies between individuals. This enabled man, by selecting those with as many desirable and as few undesirable characteristics as possible, to 'breed in' the qualities he wanted and to 'breed out' those he did not want. By this process, and by mixing various species of wild dog, he succeeded in producing an amazing variety of breeds adapted to many different purposes. In view of their descent from a rather horrible collection of wild dogs, the many useful, courageous, yet gentle animals among domestic dogs constitute one of the best examples of man's achievement as a breeder.

Arising from this is a point too often overlooked. In breeding any class of livestock or plants one must constantly guard against the tendency to revert to the wild state. Breeders cannot simply produce a breed or a strain to suit a particular purpose then sit back complacently. They must be constantly on the watch to ensure that desirable qualities are handed on and that undesirable ones are not allowed to creep back. This means that those who used dogs for specific purposes bred, not just from dogs which could work, but from dogs which *excelled* at their jobs. Those which were no good were discarded, and this policy, still practised by nearly all breeders of working dogs, has almost certainly been followed since prehistoric man first tamed the wild dog.

Of all the factors possessed by the wild dog perhaps the most important to man were its natural instincts, some beneficial, some not. Without knowledge of instincts you will never acquire that 'dog sense' so necessary for a successful man-and-dog partnership. All animals, including humans, have instincts; some tend to weaken or die with domestication, but Nature's law of survival prevents that happening in the wild state. An example is the instinct of the new-born puppy to suck its dam and to keep on squirming until it finds where the milk comes from.

An instinct might, therefore, be described as some driving force which makes an animal, without previous training or experience, want to do something. Usually, though not invariably, the following of an instinct creates pleasure. For this reason, if the opportunity to use it arises, the instinct becomes progressively stronger. It should also be noted that the strength of various instincts fluctuates between individuals of the same breed, enabling man, by selective breeding, to strengthen those he wants and weaken those he does not want. Any instinct may in fact be completely lacking. Although in the wild state a puppy that will not suck, or a dog that will not hunt, dies before it can leave any progeny, under domestication a dog lacking an instinct can live *and* be bred from.

The Hunting Instinct

There seems little doubt that the first use to which man put the dog was to help him to catch his own food, and it is, therefore, almost certain that the first domestic dogs were bred from the true hunting wild dogs. It is equally probable that the dogs found most amenable to training were those which had lived in packs, obeying the laws of a leader. For those reasons, the hunting and pack instincts are by far the strongest which have been handed down. The existence and survival of the true hunting species depended on ability to catch prey, which they were able to do by combining intelligence, speed, stamina and an acute sense of smell. These qualities would be, I think, the first to appeal to man. And right up to the present day the dog's intelligence, agility and the ability to use his nose have been three of the chief factors contributing to the high position he holds as a servant of mankind.

So much, briefly, for the hunting instinct in the wild dog, but what really concerns us is the hunting instinct in the domestic dog.

Hounds. The first use to which man put the dogs that he domesticated was hunting, and from them he bred dogs that could hunt even better. These dogs were hounds, which historians tell us have existed, practically unchanged, for many thousands of years. Right up to the present day they have been used in the same ways as they were used by primitive man. Some, such as Greyhounds and Salukis, were bred for speed, to hunt what they could see. Others, such as Foxhounds and Beagles, were bred for stamina and scenting ability to track down their quarry. Some hunted singly, some in packs, but all were bred to hunt and kill. Many became faithful companions and guardians of the home, but they were not originally bred for that purpose. In those days, if a hound could not hunt it is more than likely that it was destroyed as something useless and it would certainly never have been used for breeding.

Terriers. All the animals which man wanted to catch with dogs could not be caught by big dogs, as some lived amongst rocks, in holes in the ground, etc. So little dogs known as terriers were bred. Often they had to tackle ferocious animals bigger than themselves, and if they could not kill their quarry they had to hold it at bay until their master arrived. These little dogs had therefore to be tough.

As man domesticated other animals, dogs that wanted to chase and kill everything were bound to be a nuisance. It would appear that this was overcome at an early stage by training, but with nothing like the success achieved in producing dogs to hunt. This was only natural as, on the one hand, man was merely accentuating something that was already there, whereas, on the other, he was trying to suppress that instinct by training. Some could be taught to differentiate between wild and domestic animals, others could not. While a hound or a terrier that was a poor hunter would be destroyed, one that was a good hunter but which would kill domestic animals could be kept under control by force. It would also be used for breeding to propagate its good working qualities.

Herding Breeds. Soon man wanted dogs to help him to herd sheep and cattle. The uninitiated would expect that a dog suitable for this purpose would have to be very different from one bred to hunt, but that is not so. Many hunting dogs will make a wide detour to head off their quarry and, when dogs are hunting in packs, the fastest members often head off the quarry and turn it back to those coming up behind. If dogs that showed a tendency to head off and turn their quarry could be encouraged to head off sheep and cattle they would, indeed, be very useful. The snag would be that they would tend to catch hold and worry sheep, although they could do much less damage to cattle. This was overcome by training and by breeding from dogs with a marked tendency to head off their 'quarry' and with as little desire as possible to kill.

In this way the herding breeds were formed into a varied collection, probably the most useful of all groups today. It is important to remember, however, that the instinct to catch a quarry has never been entirely bred out and that, although some sheepdogs show no inclination to 'grip', in the majority it is kept under control only by *training*. Amazing stories are told of the sagacity of sheepdogs, but it is often overlooked that these are 'educated' dogs working under supervision. These dogs would never show any inclination to work at all if it were not for the instinct to herd, derived from the instinct to hunt. The gap between the winner of the International Sheepdog Trials 'eyeing' his sheep into the pen and the wolf or fox stalking his prey is not nearly so wide as people imagine. The Border Collie and the tame Fox in Plate I both stalk the rabbit in response to the hunting instinct. The one has been bred and trained not to attack. The other is prevented from doing so by a lead. Most domestic rabbits reared with dogs that never harm them lose their instinctive fear of this beast of prey. This one trusts all dogs. Contrary to common belief, sheepdogs are not trained either by seeing an old dog or by being tied to it (not the good ones, anyhow). They 'start to run' instinctively, and many well-bred Border Collie puppies will 'work' fowls when only a few weeks old.

In short, all the herding breeds were *bred* to herd. How to herd, what to herd and what not to herd can be learnt only by training.

Gundogs. These breeds are divided into Retrievers, Spaniels, Setters and Pointers, and there are several varieties of each. With the exception of Retrievers, all have been bred to find and flush game. Theoretically, Retrievers have been bred only to find game that has been shot and to retrieve it. I say theoretically as many people train Retrievers to work like Spaniels.

For our purpose, therefore, we can take it that *all* gundogs will hunt and flush game without any training at all. This instinct obviously comes directly from the hunting instinct of the wild dog, without modification, except that, as with hounds and terriers, it has been strengthened by selective breeding.

But a Spaniel that goes yip-yip-yip-yipping after rabbits is an abomination. A gundog that 'chases fur' is not tolerated in the best shooting circles. Any gundog puppy, however, that is any good at all will chase rabbits, hares or anything else, willy-nilly. A good gundog will flush game, then stop dead in his tracks and watch it run or fly away. This is achieved only by training.

From the hunting instinct also originates one of the most useful of all instincts in the domestic dog, the instinct to retrieve. The wild hunting dog, not to be confused with the scavenging types, rarely eats its prey on the spot but carries it off to its den. Man has developed this instinct for his own use. There seems little comparison between the fox which carries off a duck and the police dog which picks up something dropped by a criminal, but both actions arise from the same instinct. Although it is only gundog breeders who have bred specifically for this instinct, it is by no means confined to those breeds. It is rare to find a dog of any breed in which the instinct to retrieve cannot be aroused, either in play or by skilled training.

It is important to note that a hound or a terrier is often a good worker without any training at all. One has only to let them go and the hunting instinct does the rest. In a sheepdog or a gundog, however, training is all-important; the dog having to be completely under control without being held in any way. For that reason, in the breeding of the latter groups it was essential to select dogs which, apart from the instinct to work, had a natural desire to please their master. In hounds or terriers the first, and often the only, essential is the instinct to hunt.

Effects of the hunting instinct. We have now got four groups of dogs, all bred from a variety of wild dogs whose existence depended on hunting ability. These groups form practically the whole of our domestic dog population. The few breeds which cannot be fitted into any of them have been produced from them by selective breeding and/or crossing between those groups.

In bygone days, and in some parts of the world today, dogs were and are bred solely as savage guards, and I believe that several breeds regarded as sheepdogs abroad are used primarily to protect flocks against two- and four-legged enemies and not to herd as we know it in this country. Many of those dogs are too aggressive to be suitable as household companions, or, for that matter, as police dogs. In Britain, dogs which would attack anyone on sight have not been bred for a long time, and breeds once valued for their ability to rip a man to pieces have, fortunately, lost much of their aggressiveness. In any case, their numbers are so small that we may say that most dogs in this country belong to, or have been bred from, the hound, terrier, herding or gundog breeds, or from a mixture of those breeds. These include, of course, the Toy Breeds, many of which have lost little of the instincts of their working ancestors.

The instincts of these groups are not clearly divided. Given the chance, practically any dog will chase rabbits. I have had Border Collies that would set a pheasant in a bush just like a Setter, and I have seen a Springer Spaniel working poultry and showing just as much 'eye' as a Border Collie.

I come into contact with the owners of many dogs that have got into trouble, and generally the trouble is due to the owners' ignorance of what I have so far said. Quite often the dog has been chasing sheep. The owner says 'I just can't understand it. He is *such* a sweet-natured little dog and so good with the children.' To a dog there is nothing wrong in chasing anything. The young dog which chases sheep may be compared to the young man who casts his eye in the direction of a pretty girl passing by. He may even decide to walk in the same direction! Although the outcome may be quite unpredictable, he will certainly not be sentenced to death for 'doing what comes naturally' as happens to many dogs.

Once I had a sweet-natured young Corgi bitch who had never seen poultry. One day I missed her and, not being one of these people who just says 'Oh, she'll come back,' I went to investigate. In a folding unit which housed a hundred four-week-old pullets I found her—with fifty-five of them dead! She gave me a great welcome, tail wagging, eyes beaming, as if to say, 'Just look what I've done!'

Well! When I had recovered my breath, I seized the opportunity, and the bitch, and 'explained' that my dogs did not do such things. For some time after I gave her daily lessons in not chasing poultry. She completely gave up the idea and I kept her for the remainder of her life with no further trouble.

The question is not why should such a sweet-natured dog do a thing like that, but why she should not. Had she killed fifty-five rats I should have done no end of bragging about it, but how was she to know that these funny little black things should not be killed too? There and then I had to give her a terrible scolding and shaking to prevent this becoming a habit, but doing so hurt me just as much as it did her. Training has its unpleasant aspects, one being that often severe correction has to be applied when, from the dog's point of view, there has been no crime.

Here we come to a typical example of human ingratitude. From Nature man took the dog, well equipped to kill other animals, and from it he developed *for his own use* various breeds, all with a strong instinct to chase. But modern man has become less dependent on the dog as a means of obtaining his food. Unlike his predecessors, however, who developed breeds to

suit different purposes, modern man has not attempted to produce dogs for the purpose for which the majority are wanted
today—as pets. Instead, he has taken these breeds as they were
and expects them to settle down under modern conditions. The
number which, in fact, do adapt themselves to those conditions
is, to me, nothing short of amazing. But in many cases the
attempt, usually most unsuccessful, is to try to put a square
peg in a round hole. All too often the dog which follows the
instinct so carefully bred into him by man is labelled as a
'killer' and sentenced to death. The real culprit is the owner
for having allowed it to kill.

Of course, dogs can be educated, but how many are?
People will go to endless trouble to educate sons and daughters,
but will grudge spending ten or fifteen minutes a day on training their dog. Those children, as they grow up, will certainly
not all be paragons; many will follow their own instincts and
inclinations, knowing perfectly well that what they do is wrong
and can only lead to trouble. The dog, however, with no
education at all, is expected not only to know right from wrong
but invariably to do what is right. Could anything be more
unreasonable?

It seems sad that the very quality which first appealed to
man in the wild dog, and the one he has carefully cultivated
for centuries, is now the cause of more trouble than all other
factors put together. Alone, or in conjunction with the pack
instinct, the hunting instinct, in a direct or modified form, is
responsible for every case of sheep and poultry worrying, car-
chasing, cat killing, bicycle chasing and often of children being
bitten when playing with their dog.

The chief difficulty which presents itself to the prospective
dog owner is the impossibility of telling the strength of the
hunting instinct by just looking at a dog. At the regular auctions
shrewd men pay many hundreds of pounds for young Greyhounds, 'guaranteed untried', hoping to make fortunes on the
race-track or coursing field. These experienced buyers can
usually determine whether a dog is *built* on the right lines to
be fast; they can tell by his pedigree whether he is *bred* on the
right lines to be fast. What they cannot tell is whether the dog
will *try* to run faster than the others; which he will only do
provided the hunting instinct is strong enough. If these experts

cannot tell the strength of this instinct by looking at a dog, you need not even try.

Obviously the hunting instinct cannot show itself in puppies until they are at least old enough to run about. It does not usually show until much later. The first signs are generally seen in puppies at play. I have always derived the greatest interest and pleasure from studying the way in which the different instincts present themselves in puppies bred for special purposes. Terrier puppies will 'worry' each other when quite small and, as early as eight weeks, have sometimes to be separated to avoid serious fights. Greyhound puppies will chase each other, taking it in turns to be the 'hare'. Unlike terriers, they rarely try to 'kill' but merely run until exhausted, then all collapse in a heap to sleep it off—and start all over again. Gundog puppies persist in retrieving anything and everything they can carry. Collie puppies will, when quite tiny, often 'work' each other, creeping just as an adult dog in a trial does at a sheep. Corgi puppies at play show more tendency to 'heel' one another than to 'worry' as do terrier puppies.

From these small and often amusing beginnings the hunting instinct, in its various forms, develops, but the age at which it shows varies considerably. I have known Collie puppies 'start to run' at about two to three months, while others, later good workers, showed no promise until fifteen to eighteen months. Speaking very generally, the earlier an instinct makes itself apparent the stronger it is likely to be when fully developed.

At the age when the hunting or any other instinct is developing the young dog appears to have a tremendous urge to do something. He is not always sure what he wants to do, but he wants to do *something*, and anything is better than nothing. It is during this phase that most dogs are either made or marred. The trainer may succeed in starting a dog on the path which he wants it to take, then it becomes progressively easier to keep it there. Alternatively, the dog may succeed in starting on the path its instincts tell it to take, then it becomes progressively more difficult to get it back on to the 'straight and narrow'.

It is at this stage that most trainers of working dogs do everything they can to encourage the instincts they want, at the same time discouraging unwanted ones. The amount of encouragement or discouragement depends, firstly, on the strength of the instinct in the particular dog and, secondly, on the purpose for which the dog is wanted.

A well-developed instinct is essential in a good working dog, but when it gets out of control the results may be disastrous. To develop an instinct *and* keep it under control requires not only skill on the part of the trainer but work for the dog—real, practical work which you, the pet dog owner, cannot provide.

Before considering what you can do about it let us discuss what most people do at this stage.

(1) They do nothing, allowing a dog all the freedom it wants, maintaining that control is unnatural. Some even encourage instincts which are liable to get out of hand and think it funny to see their dog chasing rabbits or cats. Then they wonder why he chases sheep or poultry. By doing what comes naturally a dog develops various instincts which, if not controlled, may get completely out of hand.

(2) The dog shows a tendency to chase something, the owner becomes alarmed and thereafter keeps it shut up at home and on a lead when out. The effect is that the dog has no outlet for his energy and initiative, now at its peak. He frets, becomes 'difficult' and in many cases the balance of the mind is upset. The keener a worker the dog would make the more liable is he to be driven 'round the bend' by having nothing to do.

What, then, should you do? The dog, really a most accommodating animal, is only too willing to co-operate. Although at this stage his urge is to follow his instincts and to do the things he has been bred to do, he will be delighted to do *anything*. The only thing he does not want to do is *nothing*. By teaching him to do something, no matter how unnatural or artificial, you may not provide an outlet for his instincts, but you will provide one for at least some of his initiative. If an instinct is *never* allowed to develop it will, once this phase has reached its climax, weaken and may, in time, die out.

This point I have studied with many different dogs. For many years I bred Corgis and used them to work cattle and sheep. But circumstances changed and for a long time I had neither sheep nor cattle to work. The herding instinct, at one time such an asset to me, then became more of a nuisance, as it

PLATE I

THE HUNTING INSTINCT
The fox controlled by force, the collie by training

PLATE II

CONTRASTING EXPRESSIONS—CONTRASTING CHARACTERS

(a) Ivan, the author's well-known Alsatian

(b) Virginia McKenna, one of the stars in the M.G.M. British production *The Barretts of Wimpole Street*, with the author's Flush

(c) Dogs and cats should not be natural enemies
(*Sally Anne Thompson*)

usually is to the pet dog owner. Practically all my Corgi puppies at some stage or another went through a phase of wanting to work—in other words, of trying to round up and nip the heels of everything they could get at. As I did not want them to work there was no need to develop the instinct *and* keep it under control, so I took the much easier course of suppressing it right from the start.

In the first place the puppy gradually refrains from chasing, as he learns by experience that he must not. But he still wants to do so and, at the least relaxation on the part of whoever is in charge, he will be into the heels of a horse or goat, or scattering the ducks all over the place. By checking him *every* time, the stage is reached when the dog takes little or no interest in the animals it once wanted to chase so much.

I have conducted several little experiments to see whether, after this stage has been reached, the instinct to work could be redeveloped. In some I found that, by giving the apparently dead embers a good rake-up, the fire could easily be rekindled. In others I found this more difficult, requiring much more encouragement, and in some I was unable to get even a slight flicker. In some dogs, which I knew would have worked had their urge to do so been cultivated when it first made itself apparent, the instinct had died out completely.

In rekindling this flame I have found that it starts off with a flicker, when it wants a good deal of encouragement, then suddenly, often quite unexpectedly, it flares into a roaring fire. What is far more important is that once it has really got going this fire *cannot be put out*. Once developed, that instinct will never die or weaken. A dog with a strong working instinct will, given the opportunity, work literally to its dying day. I have known many working dogs—Terriers, Gundogs, Greyhounds, Sheepdogs—which had been retired. Some of these dogs had had no opportunity to work for years but, when the opportunity arose, had the instinct weakened? On the contrary, so far as gundogs and sheepdogs are concerned, the greatest difficulty in restarting them after a long spell is not to get them to work but to keep them under control!

It is easy to assume that a dog which takes little or no interest in livestock will not chase anything. To show how wrong that assumption may be, I shall tell you about Judy, the

c

Border Collie seen on Plate 1. She belonged to a dealer who assured me that she had been a good worker but had been living for some time as a pet in London. His attempts to get her to work were completely negative and she was obviously afraid of him. I liked the look of her, however, and bought her, mainly because I felt sorry for her but also hoping that she might work for me.

When I got her home I found that she was very friendly. I should think she had been played with a lot, probably by children, as she was *very* noisy and showed great enthusiasm in chasing a ball, retrieving sticks, etc. So far as the livestock on the place were concerned, she just ignored them and, when I tried to get her excited, she barked madly at *me*, ignoring the animals completely. One day, after about a week, I got her up as near as I could to three wild bantams and gave them a great 'shoo!' which sent them flying all over the place. Like a flash Judy was 'running wide', right round the edge of the field as far away from the bantams as possible. When she got behind them she lay down, without any word of command, chin on the ground, 'eyeing' the birds and perhaps wondering what on earth she should do next! I tried to encourage her to come on by talking to her; she started creeping towards them, getting more and more excited, and, for the first time in my life, I saw a dog creeping and barking at the same time. A 'strong-eyed' dog is normally completely silent in its work but Judy had been allowed, perhaps encouraged, to bark when excited and was now creeping instinctively and barking with excitement.

That was sufficient to show me that here was a little bitch with latent talent only waiting to be developed. I proceeded to train her and she proved a very keen and stylish worker.

There are several points of interest in this story which might apply to many dogs under similar conditions. Here is a bitch, bred from good working ancestors, from which she had inherited a strong herding instinct. It is safe to assume that this instinct had, at some stage before I had her, wanted to develop, without being able to find any outlet. (In spite of the seller's story about her having been a good worker I don't believe she had ever worked at all.) It is probable that it was then that children found her only too willing and anxious to join in their games. The herding instinct, however, had no opportunity of developing and in consequence had weakened, but it had not died. It was too strong in the first place ever to die out completely. It simply lay there, like the embers of a fire, ready to be fanned into a flame at any time. Had it had no encouragement it might never have shown, but once it had been developed, Judy seized every opportunity to work the ducks she originally ignored.

I have never known a case where the hunting instinct, once developed in any of its forms, either by the dog itself or by training, has died out. By training it can be controlled, but in all good working dogs the desire to work, once developed, always remains.

Even more important is the fact that, without an actual test, it is impossible to tell whether or not the instinct to chase is there, or how strong it is, if present. Without a test no one can tell whether this instinct is present in active form (when it may or may not be possible to control by training), in latent form (which may remain latent throughout the dog's life or may suddenly flare up as a result of some contributory cause), or whether it is absent altogether (either as a result of having died or from having been wanting in the first place).

The same principle applies to all instincts. The retrieving instinct, for instance, makes itself apparent in puppies which carry things about. They may be encouraged by the owner simply throwing an object, but a puppy cannot be made to retrieve in that way; it can only be persuaded, which means that it will retrieve only when so inclined. Provided, however, that the instinct is strong enough in the first place and is cultivated by training, it will make the dog always want to retrieve. Few gundogs are, in fact, taught to retrieve; the instinct is merely cultivated and controlled by training. The same applies to many pets, the difference being that the instinct is *not* always kept under control by training.

This instinct, as with the herding instinct, must be cultivated when it is developing in the dog. If a puppy is checked when picking things up it may lose interest in retrieving. Later on, when the owner suddenly decides that he would like the dog to retrieve, he may find that the instinct has died.

The hunting instinct does not show when a dog is lying by

the hearth. Many hounds, for instance, are the most gentle, affectionate and apparently lazy animals when kept indoors as pets—when they *are* indoors! The owner of a dog with a strong instinct to chase, however, is usually soon reminded of its presence, though it is surprising how many people fail to recognize this instinct. I have had letters with remarks such as 'I take him to the training class and he does all the exercises up to Test A very well, but when I take him to the park and he sees a dog or person in the distance, he is away! Once he has investigated, he usually comes back.' The answer is simply that when a dog sees anything moving its instinct says, 'That might be worth chasing!' When he finds that it is not worth chasing he goes back to his master. Had it been anything that would run away the dog would almost certainly have pursued it.

That is an example of an instinct that can be seen, but the evil you can see is usually less than the evil you cannot see. What cannot be seen is whether this instinct is present in latent form. The only safe policy is to assume that *every* dog will chase if given the opportunity. It is the responsibility of every dog owner to see that it does not.

Until now we have discussed the instinct to chase and how it can be developed deliberately, but in most cases where it causes trouble the instinct has developed quite accidentally. This is usually due to lack of understanding of the circumstances likely to lead to its development. Consequently, many owners who could avoid these circumstances fail to do so until too late. By far the commonest cause is too much freedom, combined with boredom.

The Pack Instinct

The next instinct, handed down from the wild dog, one which has a great influence on the domestic dog, is the pack instinct. Most wild dogs hunted in packs, and man bred some of the domestic breeds to hunt that way too. The pack (or herd) instinct is by no means peculiar to dogs; it is to be found in many other animals and in human beings. There should, therefore, be little difficulty in understanding this instinct, but it is astonishing how many people will wonder *why* a dog did the very thing they themselves would have done in the same circumstances. Most people will face danger in the company of others which they would rarely face alone. Many a quiet, well-behaved young man at home is a very different sort when out with 'the boys'! Some people are born leaders, while others are far happier with someone to follow. The same can be said of the dog, but to the pet owner the instinct to do things in a pack is far more of a nuisance than a help. A dog in a pack and the same dog on its own are two entirely different animals. With few exceptions, such as packs of hounds, man wants a dog as an individual rather than as a member of a pack and the pack instinct, if allowed to develop, can lead to endless trouble.

Nearly all dogs will chase but many will not kill what they chase. In this respect the domestic dog differs from its wild ancestor which kills its prey and either eats it on the spot or carries it off to a safe hiding-place. The domestic dog has been bred to hunt to such an extent that it chases for the sake of chasing. But although this aspect of the hunting instinct has become stronger the instinct to kill seems to have become weaker. Even a Greyhound, bred exclusively to hunt for longer than anyone knows, often refuses to kill its first hare, although it is seldom that one refuses to chase.

Most people have seen a young dog chasing a cat. When the cat stops the dog stops. The dog may even bark and pounce in an effort to get the cat to run and the game may appear to be quite harmless. Now let us take two dogs, and what better fun for two 'sporty types' than to chase a cat! The cat gives them a good run and then stops, but what do *two* dogs do? They will almost certainly attack. That is the first flicker of flame, and unless stamped right out before it gets a hold, either or both dogs may become incurable cat-killers.

Many owners are apt to say: 'Bonzo loves taking himself for a walk. He is quite safe with livestock; we have poultry of our own and he never looks at the sheep down the road.' What such people overlook is that when Bonzo and Fido, who, on his own, is just as reliable with livestock, pal up together they become two *entirely different animals*. I cannot over-emphasize the difference between a dog on its own and the same dog in a pack.

I often meet people who believe that dogs can be taught to

do almost anything by simply watching an older trained dog. If that were true how easy life would be for people like myself! There is nothing so simple as that in training dogs, but young dogs do appear to copy other dogs, young and old. This has nothing to do with intelligence. In no case does a dog say to itself, 'Well, that's a clever dog. If I do that I'll be clever too.' When one dog appears to be copying another it is merely being influenced by the pack instinct. For that reason dogs will copy each other only in things they do as a pack. Anyone who thinks that taking a dog to a training class, to see how well-trained dogs behave, will make the least bit of difference to its future behaviour must have a minus quantity of dog sense.

As an example of how this pack instinct can be used, we will consider sheepdogs and the common idea that they learn by watching a trained dog. First of all, those who train these dogs seriously rarely allow a young one to follow an old one, believing (as I do) that they will learn only bad habits. In a well-bred young dog the herding instinct should be strong enough to make him want to 'run' without outside encouragement. It does happen, however, that some young dogs show little or no inclination to 'run'. These can quite often be encouraged by allowing them to follow an older dog. This is not due to copying but to the pack instinct arousing the instinct to chase. Of course, sheepdogs should not kill or even grip, and here we come to the reason why trainers do not, as a rule, let a young dog follow an old one. The pack instinct tends to weaken the instinct to herd and to strengthen the instinct to hunt and kill. As a result, the youngster will not stay with the trained dog and keep away from the sheep, but will want to go in and grip, one of the commonest faults that has to be eradicated even when the pack instinct is not present.

If, instead of a young and an old dog, we take two untrained young ones, neither of which shows much inclination to 'run', they will almost certainly encourage each other to do so. In this case, however, neither is trained, so both will simply follow the pack and herding instincts, but the former will so strengthen the true hunting instinct that the herding instinct will be overruled. The most likely result is that the youngsters will tear round a flock of sheep until they get them up in a bunch, when they will grab hold of one and probably start worrying it.

I hope I have not given the impression that whenever two dogs get together they will worry everything they see, or that a lot of dogs together cannot be kept under control. For many years now my wife and I have kept a pack of dogs which gives us an opportunity to study the pack instinct at first hand. We have also kept, and still keep, a wide variety of animals including, at the time of writing, some twenty cats which have the complete freedom of the place. Amongst our pack of dogs (also around twenty in number) are several which were inveterate cat chasers before we had them at ages ranging from two to four years. But they all potter about amongst the cats on the most friendly terms. Or so it appears. But if we were to assume that this was due to friendship rather than tolerance we would soon be in trouble. Some of the dogs really are friendly with some of the cats. But the real reason why they all get on so well is because we, the pack leaders, do not think it at all funny to see dogs chasing cats and we stamp firmly on the slightest inclination to do so. Although our dogs are allowed a great deal of freedom they are never allowed *complete* freedom. They are like a class of children when the teacher has gone out of the class room. They won't get up to much mischief so long as they think the teacher is likely to reappear unexpectedly. But the longer they are left the more likely is trouble to start and it always starts with a ringleader—a pack leader.

So we never leave our dogs for any length of time on their own. Some we can safely leave for quite a long time but others we shut up if we have to leave them at all. If we did not do this it is almost certain that one day one dog would set about a cat (probably to tease rather than to chase) which would retaliate. This would be taken as a cue for the others to join in and, in less time than it takes to write, we would have a pack of cat killers. And, of course, a dead cat, which alive could be more valuable to us than any of the dogs. We have trained many individual dogs not to chase cats and could no doubt teach most of the pack not to chase cats on their own. But once a *pack* had killed a cat I doubt very much if it could be broken of killing others. With the pet dog too it is always so much simpler to prevent an instinct developing than to try to control it once it has developed.

I use the cat as an example of 'prey' to a dog because for

many years we have had a lot of cats mingling with a lot of dogs, giving us the opportunity of studying their behaviour at first hand. I also use it because of the prevalent idea that dogs and cats are natural enemies. This is absolute rubbish. Nor is there any reason why cats and dogs should be natural enemies as both are predators. A dog will chase poultry, sheep or another dog as readily as a cat and a pack of two is very likely to kill or severely injure the quarry. There have been cases of people who screamed and/or ran from a pack of dogs being severely mauled and even unfortunate cases of small children being killed. This is not due to the dog being savage or having 'a nasty streak in him' but simply to an instinct getting out of hand. The more I see of the way dogs are treated the more surprised I become as to how few accidents there are.

There are two main reasons why so many dogs chase cats. Firstly pet dogs usually have access to cats more readily than other animals and, because they have been chased, most cats will run from a dog. But the chief cause of the 'cat and dog' falacy undoubtedly arises from the hunting instinct of the majority of *dog owners*. It is dog owners, not dogs, which are the natural enemies of cats. For some inexplicable reason they regard the cat as fair game for their dog although it is a domestic animal, brought up to trust mankind and possibly just as much a friend to their neighbour as the dog is to them. To make this attitude all the more illogical many of these dog owners are actively 'anti blood sports'!

To show how strong the pack instinct is, I must mention what is quite the most horrible trait that has been handed down from the wild dog. I refer to the instinct to kill off the aged, infirm and weak members of the pack, resulting in dogs being killed in kennel fights. Two dogs start a scrap, the rest of the pack join in and in no time there is a ghastly fight. If dogs were 'almost human' they would take sides, each going to the aid of its friend, but that does not happen. Instead, they all attack the 'weakling', which may have had no part in starting the trouble. To separate two dogs fighting is difficult; to break up a pack fight is impossible without the aid of one or two *experienced* people. If the fight is broken up, and the 'weakling' escapes with a bad chewing, the pack, now that the instinct has been aroused, will seize every opportunity of having another go. To make matters worse, the poor victim is usually terrified, and the more terrified it appears, the more anxious are the others to finish it off. This means that it cannot be allowed out with the others again as a pack, although it may get on all right with several of them as individuals.

'Horrible!' you say, and what often makes it more horrible is that the 'weakling', which the pack decides has reached the age when it is of no further use, is very often an old favourite. 'Only dogs with a nasty streak in them would do that sort of thing' you may think, but here you would be quite wrong. I have seen some of the most friendly and affectionate dogs transformed into savage wild animals as a result of this pack-fighting instinct. This shows just how strong a dormant and *apparently* non-existent instinct can be. Considering that man has never tried to preserve this instinct and that it may not show itself for several generations, you should realize how strong those instincts which have been carefully cultivated and preserved from generation to generation can be.

CHAPTER II

GUARDING INSTINCT AND FIGHTING

Advantages and disadvantages

THE dog's instinct to guard master and property is, no doubt, an asset to a wider range of dog owners than any other instinct. Unfortunately, however, it frequently becomes a liability, resulting in many dogs being continually shut or tied up, or being sentenced to death, the latter being the lesser evil. The dog's instinct is not only to protect himself but also to protect the remainder of the pack, its home and anything belonging to it. This instinct has been preserved in varying degrees, and most dogs have some instinct to guard, irrespective of breed. Some breeds and some strains, of course, produce more good guards than others, and many of our native working breeds produce just as many as some of the imported breeds with their wonderful reputations.

Many people have peculiar ideas as to the essential qualities of a good guard. Most have heard of trained guard dogs which will attack on command, but, although these are of very real use to Service men and in the guarding of factories, etc., I do not recommend them for the ordinary householder, for, in the hands of a novice, such an ally is likely to be a greater danger than the enemy. But in these days of cosh attacks I do not think the value of a good natural guard is fully appreciated. Some people appear to regard as a good guard a dog that is ready to tear the throat out of every stranger. If a dog is going to live in a civilized community it must behave in a civilized way, and no dog should ever bite anyone unless provoked. The good guard has no desire to attack but merely to protect. Many of the best guards are the most friendly and sweet-natured animals with those they know and trust.

The job of a good guard should always be defensive, never offensive, and here I might contradict the erroneous idea that police dogs are savage. For civilian police purposes (Army and

R.A.F. dogs are in a different category) the first essential is that the dog must bite only as a last resort; in the schedule of Police Dog Trials it is stated that 'every unnecessary bite will be penalized'. The necessity for this should be obvious, as the dog that apprehends an armed thug may also be expected to find a lost child.

It is not, however, in the police dog that we are interested, but in one that will protect your house, family and yourself. To do that a dog need not be aggressive. Here we come to a sort of sixth sense which I consider many dogs have—a sense of danger. Most people have heard of dogs that take an inexplicable dislike to a person, who, it later transpires, was up to no good.

The wife or child of a gamekeeper or shepherd when going out after dark invariably takes a dog. Not a trained guard dog, not an imported foreign breed, but just an ordinary gundog or sheepdog. If, during the course of a day's work, that dog attacked an innocent person, the owner would be more than annoyed. If, however, the dog allowed anyone to molest his wife or child he would probably shoot it. It is unlikely that this would happen, as the guarding instinct, combined with danger, would almost certainly cause the dog to threaten the wrongdoer and, if necessary, to bite.

Leading police dog trainers have found that the keen dog always on the lookout for trouble, which was at one time favoured, is no better than, if as good as, the quiet, inoffensive-looking one when it comes to a real show-down. The aggressive dog has to be constantly kept under the thumb of the handler, who has more freedom to attend to other details if he knows this his dog will *not* attack until necessary but *will* attack when necessary.

In choosing a puppy, which you hope will be a good guard, the points to look for are those shown by the parents and other relations rather than by the puppy itself. Age, too, is important in deciding whether a dog is likely to be a good guard. An eight-week-old puppy that barks at strangers will probably be either shy or too aggressive when older. Little puppies should be friendly with anyone, though the extent to which they are friendly varies with upbringing. Puppies reared indoors with children are likely to be more friendly than those reared in kennels. When four or five months old a puppy will often show some guarding instinct, usually by barking at strangers, but some, which later become good guards, do not do so until they are a year or more. A dog brought up with a home of his own to guard will show the guarding instinct earlier and more enthusiastically than one brought up in kennels. Kennel dogs often make a lot of noise rather than guard properly, but that does not mean that they will not make good guards when they have a home of their own. Only a very aggressive dog, especially a young one, will show much inclination to guard on strange ground, but once it owns the place, so to speak, its attitude will change.

The first, and by far the most important, point is that a dog should stand his ground. If a young dog barks at a stranger, then goes straight up and looks him up and down, he will probably become an excellent guard. The dog that flies around screaming and barking hysterically is not worth the food he eats, and, of course, the dog that whips round the back of a stranger, has him by the leg, and then vanishes, is worse than useless. Of course a dog should bark; there is nothing more likely to deter burglars than a noisy dog, even a little one. A dog that barks, however, is no use at all if, as a stranger approaches, he hides behind you or disappears altogether. A good dog will always place itself between its owner and a stranger.

Generally speaking, the earlier the instinct shows, the stronger it is likely to be when developed. On the other hand, it can be completely lacking. It can, to some extent, be developed or suppressed by the owner. Like all instincts, it may be present in greater strength than is apparent and may easily be encouraged, quite accidentally, to flare up and get out of control.

Some dogs can be trained to attack and really bite without getting too 'hot'. They will attack *only* on command, and are quite safe. This is because the guarding instinct is strengthened by the hunting instinct or more correctly that part of the hunting instinct which makes a dog want to grab hold of something and worry it. Whether it is an old sack or a man's arm makes no difference to such a dog which is ever anxious to attack on the slightest suspicious move by the 'enemy'. Unfortunately, without putting it to the test, it is impossible to tell quite how keen a dog will become. Once the fire is lit, however, it cannot be put out and the result of the general public going about with such dogs would be that a gentleman raising his hat to a lady would run the risk of finding his arm in the grip of her dog!

The Desire to Fight. From the guarding instinct comes the desire to fight other dogs, usually stronger in the male than in the female. Bitches, however, will fight, and when they do they are often far more difficult to separate than dogs. If two bitches develop a dislike for each other they rarely get over it, whereas two dogs will scrap today and be pals tomorrow. Although the instinct to fight arises from the guarding instinct, it does not follow that the best guards are inevitably the worst fighters, or that the dog which attacks other dogs on sight will also want to attack humans. Although the dog appears willing, even anxious, to accept a human master in place of a canine pack leader, its reactions to people are quite different to its reactions to other members of its species or to other animals. Dogs that fight for the sake of fighting are often grand dogs in every other way, and almost invariably wonderful with children. I have also known excellent guards which showed no inclination to fight.

To the owner this tendency to fight may be anything from a confounded nuisance to an absolute menace. In practically all working breeds, fighting has always been regarded as a serious fault and few of their breeders will breed from a known fighter.

I often hear people praising a dog that fights, or wants to fight, on the grounds that it shows 'guts'. That is not necessarily so. Fighting dogs can roughly be divided into three groups: (1) those that fight for the sake of fighting, and thoroughly enjoy it; (2) those that fight because of the guarding instinct, and will only attack another dog if it approaches their master or comes on to their property; and (3) those that fight through fear. Nearly all dogs of the first two groups have 'guts' and some of the best working dogs I have known would, in inexperienced hands, undoubtedly have developed into awful fighters. The last type, however, fights because he *lacks* 'guts'; because he is afraid he tries to get one in first. As he loses his head at the sight of another dog he is the worst type and nothing can be done about it.

Both the guarding instinct and the desire to fight can be aroused by the pack instinct. Two keen guard dogs may be safe on their own but dangerous together, and two dogs, neither much good as guards, may 'egg each other on' to appear, or even be, quite ferocious.

One of our biggest problems in working or exercising dogs in public places is the possibility of the sudden appearance of uncontrolled dogs. On several occasions strange dogs have appeared in the middle of displays. People who spoke to us afterwards usually marvelled at the things the dogs did, but, when such an incident occurred, they never marvelled at what the dogs did *not* do—follow their instinct to catch, and probably kill, the intruder.

If I mention that our dogs would, if allowed, attack a strange dog, most people are surprised. On the street, or anywhere else, not one of them would dream of attacking another dog, but the greatest test of the control of our dogs occurs when a strange dog, cat or rabbit unexpectedly appears before the pack. As I have said, a dog on its own and the same dog in a pack are two *entirely* different animals.

We must *train* our dogs to keep their instincts under control; all *you* have to do is to prevent circumstances arising which are likely to lead to an accumulation of temptations to which all *real* dogs are only too willing to yield.

From what I have said in these two chapters I hope you will be able to see why, amongst other things, dogs which are 'safe with all livestock' may suddenly take to worrying sheep; why those that have previously shown no inclination to fight may suddenly become inveterate fighters. According to some people, once a dog has tasted blood he becomes an incurably savage animal. Yet the practice of feeding nothing but raw meat is becoming more and more common in kennels. I used to believe stories about sheepdogs that ate a leg of mutton and were thereby transformed into sheep-worriers until I saw an old Highland shepherd skin a lamb, born dead, and throw the warm carcase to his dog. He told me that he had done it for years to generations of dogs and had never found that the practice made any difference to a dog; he had never had one worry sheep. Tasting blood has nothing to do with it. It is simply that an instinct, hitherto inactive, is suddenly strengthened and takes control. That instinct may or may not be present in *any* dog; the only safe thing to do is to assume that it *is* there in *every* dog. If, therefore, you don't know where your dog is, go and find out—quickly! Don't just say: '*He* won't do any harm. He's such a sweet little dog.' Dogs will be dogs and neither you nor anyone else knows what they will do, if tempted. There is no temptation so easy to resist as the one which is not there. But people with an education and a religion to guide them all too often yield to the temptations which *are* there—so why shouldn't a dog?

CHAPTER III

SUBMISSIVE INSTINCT
INSTINCT OF FEAR. TEMPERAMENT

WE now come to two instincts each closely allied, in different ways, to the most important factor affecting you and your dog —*temperament*. So far I have been dealing with instincts which, in the past, were of great value to mankind; instincts, however, which make dogs more difficult to control than most other pet animals. To keep those in check training is necessary but, in this respect, the dog brings to the trainer an important ally. This is in the form of what I call the *submissive instinct*, which arises directly from the pack instinct.

Given the opportunity a young dog will often develop a friendship, sometimes amounting to a passion, for an older dog and will follow the latter in almost everything it does, but will make no attempt to do the same things on its own. But if that young dog is removed from the influence of the older dog and is taken in hand by a human being, it will form just as great a friendship for the human leader. This fact is of the greatest importance. The great German authority the late Konrad Most, in his book *Training Dogs*, based his training methods entirely on this 'pack leader' and 'member of the pack' relationship, even going to the extent of suggesting that trainers should imitate the actions of a canine leader. I prefer to raise the dog to the status of a servant rather than lower myself to that of a dog, but the principle is the same.

Although we are, in fact, dealing with an aspect of the pack instinct itself, I think it is perhaps better to say that *from* the pack instinct—the instinct to follow a leader—has been developed the submissive instinct. This might also be referred to as amenability to discipline, or a desire to please, but, as we are discussing instincts, we might as well refer to it as the submissive instinct.

To the average dog owner, this is probably one of the most important instincts for, although it has little relationship to

PLATE III

(*a*) *and* (*b*) A typical Field Trial Cocker and a show type

(*c*) Scottish Terrier Champion 1913

(*d*) Scottish Terrier Champion 1955

PLATE IV

(a) Little puppies should always run to the sound they associate with food

(b) 'No, I won't.' Simply to stand and stare will get you nowhere

what a dog can be taught, it is directly responsible for the *ease* with which it can be taught. An important point is that the strength of this submissive instinct varies tremendously between individual dogs and different breeds. The majority are pleased to have someone to guide them, but there are others, cut out to be leaders, which resent guidance and detest discipline. For some purposes a strong submissive instinct was unnecessary, while for others it was essential, and for that reason (together with the fact that in the wild pack there are leaders and followers) man, in developing various breeds for various purposes, has produced dogs with weak and strong submissive instincts. In some dogs the submissive instinct seems wholly absent, and these are impossible to train in the ordinary sense of the word.

Nearly all dogs have some submissive instinct which, like other instincts, will become stronger or weaker according to circumstances. Like the hunting instinct, it cannot be measured by simply looking at a dog, but a fair idea can be formed by studying behaviour, even in small puppies. A submissive dog likes being made a fuss of. If spoken to he will show interest, even if he is untrained and does not know what the words mean. Puppies will nearly always rush to be petted, but occasionally an independent little blighter stalks off on his own and couldn't care less about fussing. That type is likely to be difficult to train, although it often makes an excellent dog when trained—*if* trained!

It is because of this submissive instinct that, far from being cruel to train a dog, it is cruel not to do so. In the wild state the dog had a leader, but in his long association with man he has handed over that leadership to his two-legged master. Nothing gives a submissive dog greater pleasure than pleasing its master.

As an instance of this, a dog will become attached to the person who trains it, not (as is commonly believed) to the one who feeds or exercises it. Of this I am quite convinced. When I first started breeding, I was fortunate in having a mother who always fed my dogs and reared the puppies, and now I have a wife who does all the feeding and most of the exercising. The position is, therefore, that over a period of more than thirty years I have never fed my dogs and now only occasionally exercise them, but the dogs *I* train show far more affection for

D

me than for the person who feeds them. If my wife has the pack out and I appear, the ones I have trained will delightedly rush up to me. The ones I have not trained continue to amuse themselves in their own ways. If, when my wife and I have the dogs out together, we were to walk in opposite directions without calling any of them, those she has trained would go with her and those I have trained would come with me. Those which have had no individual training, such as puppies, would go with the one who has reared them.

Often we rear two or three puppies together and, when they are old enough, my wife and I decide to train one each. Until then, although friendly, as all puppies should be, they have shown no particular affection for me. The one I train, however, becomes more and more *my* dog and after a few weeks will show far more affection for me than for my wife, who still feeds it. The one my wife trains becomes even more attached to her and shows less interest in me than it did before.

The submissive instinct may be sufficiently strong to make a dog so anxious to please its owner that it is only necessary to get it to understand what is wanted for it to do it. That is rare, but, unless the submissive instinct is absent altogether (also rare), it can be developed by training. As I shall mention later, the best exercises to develop this instinct are the modern standard obedience exercises, but to teach a dog to do *anything* —to sit up and beg, give a paw or anything else—develops the instinct, so long as the dog does it when *you* tell him, not just when *he* feels like doing it.

Whether or not the instincts to which I have referred in previous chapters *can* be kept under control depends on whether the submissive instinct is strong enough to counter-balance them. If weak in the first place, it may be impossible to strengthen it enough to overpower a highly developed instinct, such as the hunting instinct; especially if the latter was allowed to develop before any attempt was made to develop the submissive instinct.

Instinct of Fear

The wild dog had some instincts which were decidedly undesirable and man was faced with the task of overcoming them. The most important was probably fear of mankind.

Practically all wild animals have an instinctive fear of man, due to the sad fact that man is their natural enemy. Fortunately, most of them, if removed from the nest when very young and reared by a human being, will attach themselves to that person in practically the same way as they would to their own parent. This, no doubt, was helpful in the early domestication of animals, but instinctive fear presented itself in degrees varying enormously between individuals. If we take as an example the two best-known species of wild dog still existing, the wolf and the fox, it will be found that cubs taken from the nest at an early age and brought up by hand will vary considerably in their attitude to humans. A few will become friendly, others will remain suspicious and often treacherous. The majority probably grow up to trust people they know but are always suspicious of strangers, often being aggressive towards them.

It is safe to assume that that is how the first domesticated wild dogs reacted. The unreliable types would be discarded, the more friendly ones kept. They did not have to be friendly towards strangers, however, and in many cases a suspicious dog would have been preferable to one that trusted every Tom, Dick and Harry. But there is a vast difference between a suspicious dog that will not allow a stranger to touch it and one that is terrified and bolts whenever it sees someone it does not know. The latter, being useless as working dogs, were no doubt discarded from the start, and by this process man bred out (to a great extent though not entirely) the instinct of fear. Unfortunately, many present-day dog breeders do not appear to believe in that policy but breed from dogs which would certainly have been shot in the old days. The result is that, while man originally produced dogs which have better temperaments than their wild ancestors, today we find an ever-increasing number that are more afraid than a wild dog would be under similar conditions. The tame fox, shown on Plate 1, has far more confidence than many dogs that I meet.

This instinct also has a sort of two-way effect. Animals that are savage or snappy will rarely attack anyone who is not afraid of them. This knowledge is of the greatest use to those who have to deal with difficult animals and, incidentally, to those who claim supernatural powers over animals. I have trained and worked all sorts of dogs and horses, good, bad and indifferent, and have also had under my care a number of bulls, mostly Ayrshires, noted for quick temper. I have also worked with people who did the same jobs—grooms, horse-breakers, herdsmen, etc. These are not the people who make newspaper headlines by claiming to be able to communicate in some mysterious way with animals. They are just ordinary people whose job of work is to look after animals.

There are few indeed who have spent their life amongst animals who have met none that was not difficult at the best of times, dangerous at the worst, but the proportion of those people who get injured is really very small. Why? Because they are not afraid. They don't tease, shout or bully. They never punish an animal unless really necessary and they never threaten; one of the commonest mistakes dog owners make.

It is possible to pretend to a dog that one is afraid (this is done when teaching guard dogs to attack) but it is not always possible to pretend that one is not. A dog will immediately realize on meeting a stranger for the first time whether or not that person is scared. There have been many cases of reputedly savage animals making no attempt to attack a child or an adult who was either mad or drunk. These people were not attacked because, not realizing the danger, they showed no fear.

Temperament

We now come to temperament, so closely allied to the two preceding instincts. It is, however, a complex characteristic involving a number of other factors.

The most important is nervousness, usually arising directly from the instinct of fear which makes a dog want to escape to the extent of biting, often viciously, like a cornered fox or a rat. This is responsible for many dogs 'losing their heads' and biting without any warning, and for practically all cases of people being bitten by their own dogs.

This type of temperament appears to be on the increase and the reasons seem fairly obvious. The fundamental one is the tendency to revert to Nature. Put briefly, this means that, as the wild dog had an undesirable temperament, it always has been and always will be easier to breed bad temperaments than good ones. By breeding from stock excelling in temperament there is always the risk that some offspring will not reach the same high standard. By breeding from nervous stock with bad temperaments, however, the possibility of getting anything better is practically nil and there is every possibility that many offspring will be worse—far worse—than their parents.

The second reason is that, although man considerably improved the temperament of the wild dog, a tendency to nervousness was not always a great disadvantage. To a shepherd, working on the hills, a dog afraid of strangers or noise might not be a handicap, but to anyone living in a town the same dog would be a bundle of nerves, of no value to its owner and a misery to itself.

In mentioning the effect of environment I should perhaps stress that temperament is not produced by upbringing, training or anything else. It is something that is *there*. It can be made better or worse but you cannot turn a bad temperament into a good one; although many people appear to have remarkable success in turning good ones into bad ones!

Another reason for the increase in bad temperaments is the belief that, to be any good as a guard, a dog must be suspicious of strangers. As I have pointed out, that is not essential and there is all the difference between suspicion and fear. The real danger lies in the fact that it is difficult to tell whether a dog is suspicious or afraid without actual test, which is often impractical. The result is that many people breed from dogs they believe to be suspicious, but which are, in fact, nervous or cowardly.

Apart from the disadvantages to yourself in owning a nervous dog, I regard it as downright cruelty to keep a really nervous dog in this modern world.

To a person suffering from 'nerves' life is often quite terrifying, but we know what it is all about, or at least can try to find out. Just imagine a poor dog, with no idea why there should be buses and cars on the streets, trains on the railways, jet 'planes and supersonic bangs in the air and screaming children everywhere, all armed with fireworks on November 5th. There are hundreds of terrified, shivering creatures dragged out into that pandemonium every day of their miserable lives, by owners who 'cannot bear to part with them'—because they are so *fond* of them! To anyone who has the misfortune to own such a dog (I do not mean a dog that is afraid merely because he is strange and unaccustomed to his surroundings), I would say it is your *duty* to have him humanely destroyed. If you refuse to do so you are being far more cruel than were many people who have been punished by law for more generally recognized acts of cruelty.

Another factor affecting temperament is temper. Many good dogs have quite a bit of temper and they can usually be made to keep it under control. There is also what might be described as quick temper, rather than bad temper, as shown by a dog that snaps at the foot that happens to tread on his toe, then immediately 'apologizes'. That type of temper cannot be controlled, it is over before the dog knows what he has done, but, on its own, it rarely presents any serious problem.

What you must guard against is the dog that is bad-tempered *and* nervous. Temper will make a dog retaliate if attacked but, when combined with nervousness, the dog will often bite through the fear that it may be going to be attacked. Such dogs may be dangerous, as are those in which a strong guarding instinct is combined with fear. The latter type instinctively want to protect but fear won't let them wait until action is necessary. A dog of this kind tries to get one in first, often biting some perfectly innocent person in the process, but will usually run away—his instinct of fear overpowers his guarding instinct—when protection is really needed.

The submissive instinct is also closely tied up with temperament, giving us what trainers call 'hard' and 'soft' dogs. The hard dog is usually bold and fearless, a leader rather than a follower—an excellent servant but an equally bad master. Invariably either one or other—there is no question of working on an equality basis. The soft dog with a highly developed submissive instinct is generally easily trained; not always so much through a desire to please as from a lack of desire to do anything on his own. A dog with an over-developed submissive instinct often lacks character, initiative, and everything that goes to make a *real* dog.

A hard dog is more difficult to train, but he usually has much more courage and initiative. He may not always do the right thing but he will at least do *something*, whereas when anything goes wrong the sensitive dog does nothing or even disappears completely! Another point is that, although one requires much more willpower and determination to train a hard dog, one does not require nearly so much patience.

It does not follow that I advise you to get a hard dog. Unless you have the time and ability to train it, my advice is definitely *not* to have such a one, as it will almost certainly get into trouble. On the other hand, it would be preferable to a nervous one, which should be avoided like the plague.

Do not overlook the significance of initiative, which in a working dog is essential. The foxhound or police dog that sticks to a cold line on a bad scenting day, or the gundog that goes on searching for a bird shot hours beforehand, is not necessarily the dog with the strongest sense of smell. In dogs, as in humans, the ability to do something is of little value without the will to do it and the dog which succeeds is the one that keeps on trying. For this reason man has gone to great pains to breed dogs with initiative. Having succeeded in doing so, we now find that many dogs possessing this quality are expected to sit around quite happily doing nothing!

Like most other factors, initiative can be encouraged or suppressed, but you cannot encourage something which is not there, or suppress something that is too strong for suppression. Some dogs are willing to accept a life of idle luxury; their initiative dies, often smothered by affection, and they become just things which lie by the fire and eat food. Most dogs, however, don't want to be 'mothers' darlings' all their lives and rebel against such treatment. They become difficult. Many bite their owners (who can blame them?) and some go insane. All because so many dog owners refuse to provide an outlet for the initiative which man has carefully preserved, even strengthened, in the dog.

In practice the most important points to note regarding temperament are: (1) to find a dog that is not nervous, bad-tempered or, worst of all, both, and (2) to find a dog that suits *you*. Some people can take a timid dog and, with infinite patience, train him. In the process they may give the dog such confidence that he will never show his natural shyness (not to be confused with downright nervousness). The blustering, impatient type of person, or a house full of rowdy children, would unbalance the mind of such a dog. It would probably be regarded as stupid, whereas in fact the sensitive dog often has exceptional intelligence; it is the owners who are too stupid to see that! So long as he does not lose his temper (no one who does should ever *attempt* to train any animal) the blustering sort will probably get on very well with a hard dog that would make a fool of anyone who likes a shy one. It is for that reason that a dog which is of no use in one home can go to another where it will be a huge success. Sometimes the people who first had him can get another dog which will be just as great a success with them. It is quite possible to find two people with equally good working dogs, which, if they were to exchange, would neither of them be any good at all.

Most of us know people who, for no reason that we can explain, get on our nerves, but few people realize just how much the same applies to dogs. Unfortunately, the poor dog's only means of telling these would-be friends exactly what he thinks of them is to bite, or to threaten to bite. For this he is usually regarded as vicious and often sentenced to death. He may not be a bit vicious, and may get on very well with other people, while the person who gets on his nerves may get on with other dogs.

There are also dogs which get on some people's nerves. If you have an excitable temperament it is more than likely that a 'jumpy' dog will irritate you. It is even more likely that you will make such a dog much worse and he will probably end up a nervous wreck. The same dog in the hands of someone placid might get over its tendency to nervousness and grow into a bold sensible animal. This important aspect of temperament is all too often overlooked.

To try to decide, on seeing a dog for the first time, what sort of temperament it has is no easy task, even for the experienced. To do so with young puppies is almost impossible, as they change considerably. Here I cannot over-emphasize the importance of the sort of temperament a dog carries in its pedigree; a matter to which I shall refer more fully later.

The first (often the only) guide is the dog's expression.

The first thing I go for is a dog that looks me straight in the face. If I am a stranger and he looks right through me, so much the better. That is what I hope he will do to strangers when I am his master but, whether I be friend or foe, he must look straight at me, *honestly*, so that I know at once whether he likes or dislikes me. The shape of the skull has some bearing on this matter, as no dog can look anyone straight in the face with both eyes if those eyes are set at an angle on the side of the head. The bold yet friendly and honest dog that I have in mind always has its eyes set fairly wide apart on a broad skull with well defined stop.

The eye I like is either oval or round, large rather than small, but not pop-eyed or with a mad, staring look. Colour can be misleading, as a light eye often looks fierce, whereas a dark one looks kind, but what would look light in a black dog would look dark, warm and kind in a white one. A black eye usually denotes a hard, often a dull, dog and, although I like a nice warm, brown eye, some of the most intelligent dogs I have known have had very light eyes. Beware of the dog with the languid 'film star' sort of eye; it is really foreign to the dog and is often deceptive. The top illustrations in Plate II are a good example of this. The bold, honest eye of the Alsatian is a true reflection of his character but the rather doleful one of the Cocker is not. Flush is, in fact, a merry little bitch, full of life. She is extraordinarily greedy and will appear to adore people she dislikes intensely if she thinks they will produce a tit-bit. Whatever you do, avoid a mean, 'piggy' expression, or the shifty, furtive look that has been handed down from the wolf or other treacherous ancestors.

The opinion formed by the dog's expression can be strengthened by studying his behaviour, remembering the purpose for which you want him and the sort of temperament *you* have. If you like a hard dog and are prepared to *make* him behave (few people do), then you need not worry if he has a hard eye or shows little inclination to please his owner. If you want a dog to train for obedience competitions or any type of work, you will want one both responsive and lively; one with a real twinkle in his eye. If he leaps up with glee and nearly knocks you over, or tows you on the lead, you need not worry, as these are faults that can easily be cured by training—when you know how. On the other hand, if he looks out of his kennel and, seeing a stranger, disappears into it again, leave him there; nervousness may, to some extent, be camouflaged by skilful training but it is rarely overcome, and a nervous dog is *never* reliable. Those who want a nice quiet family dog that will get into the minimum of trouble with the minimum of training should try to get one with a placid temperament; even at the risk of his getting a bit lethargic in his old age.

Nervousness, so important to avoid, can be difficult to identify. Dogs which are sometimes described to me as 'one-man dogs' are merely terrified of everything around them. On the other hand, people sometimes think a dog is nervous simply because he resents strangers. We had a Saluki which would back away from a stranger who tried to touch him, keeping just out of arms' reach. He would also back away as a tame rabbit approached him. Was he afraid of the rabbit? Not in the slightest. He merely knew better than to kill it. That, however, was no reason why he should lower himself to be friendly with it!

In the same way he and many similar dogs know better than to bite a stranger but, although one can teach a dog not to bite people, one cannot *make* him like them. After all, most of us know people who make us feel exactly the same. Although some people claim the ability to make friends with *any* dog, I I have yet to meet one who could prove it. That particular dog was not at all nervous and would trot gaily through a fairground in full blast.

The danger lies in the fact that on meeting a dog for the first time it is very difficult, often impossible, to be sure whether he draws back through fear or just to stop himself biting you. Great care should be taken in choosing this type of dog, but there is no reason why it should be avoided. Provided it is *not* nervous, that is, in fact, the type of dog I like as a companion.

CHAPTER IV

OTHER INSTINCTS

Sex—Cleanliness—Homing

Sex Instinct

This is the cause of more 'dog trouble' than is generally realized. Dogs worry sheep or poultry, chase cars or bite delivery boys on bikes in response to the hunting instinct. But the majority leave home in response to the sex instinct. Having left home, the dog is far more likely to find something to satisfy his hunting instinct (probably strengthened by another dog or dogs to form a pack) than to satisfy his sex instinct. Although essential if we want to have dogs, this instinct is never an asset to trainers or to anyone who owns a dog purely as a companion.

In the wild state the female comes in season once a year and at a certain time of year, so that puppies are born in the spring. Domestication has altered this; now bitches usually come in season twice a year and at any old time. That does not affect us much; what does are the changes that have taken place in the sexual instincts of the male dog.

The strength of this instinct varies very considerably between individuals, and in normal dogs it should not present any serious problem. Many dogs, however, develop varying degrees of abnormality, often becoming sex maniacs. At the other extreme, we get dogs which appear to have no sex instinct at all. Although not much help to the breeder this, of course, benefits the pet dog owner. Over-sexed dogs are, in many cases, practically impossible to train, have usually little affection for their owners and are often most embarrassing.

The reasons why such dogs are so numerous are, to me, obvious. Taking mongrels first, one can find in almost every district a dog who spends his entire life making himself a confounded nuisance to the owner of every bitch for miles around. That his efforts have not been in vain is apparent from the number of his offspring. When he gets too old to be first on the

59

doorstep, his place will probably be taken by one of his sons. Many of his daughters and grand-daughters will have found homes with irresponsible owners who allow them out when in season, and by a process of line-breeding, uncontrolled but just as effective as that practised by pedigree stock breeders, we find local 'strains' of mongrels with only one instinct—sex— developed to any extent. Many of these dogs are cunning rather than intelligent and this cunning they use in following their one-track mind.

That sort of thing does not happen with pedigree dogs, but something just as bad does, which, as it is done deliberately, is all the greater discredit to pedigree dog breeders. A great many dogs are kept solely for the money they earn in stud fees. No normal dog would mate the number of bitches that these dogs do, and many dogs advertised as 'wonderful stud dogs' are, in fact, sex maniacs. 'Like father, like son' applies to dogs, which is all very well for those whose sole object in keeping a dog is to earn stud fees. The majority of dogs, however, do not reach a sufficiently high standard to be of any value at stud. These are the ones usually sold as pets. If you keep your dog at home, as everyone should, he will obviously have no outlet for his sexual instincts. In a normal dog this appears to have no ill-effects, but in an over-sexed dog constant frustration can lead to mental derangement, often ending in complete lunacy.

This instinct does not, in my opinion, flare up with use or die down by being left idle. I have worked many dogs, some of which were used at stud a lot, some only occasionally, some not at all. Some were used before training, while others were trained and had been working for some time before being used, but in spite of careful observation I have been unable to find proof that to use or not to use a normal dog at stud makes the slightest difference to its temperament or behaviour.

The sex instinct is always present, whether used or not, but many young dogs go through a phase, as with the other instincts, when this one seems very strong. During this stage there will be, amongst other things, a strong tendency to roam, whether there be a bitch in season or anything to chase making no difference. If allowed to develop, this will very soon become a habit and many dogs spend most of their lives roaming around from place to place, often miles apart, for no particular reason. A dog of this kind is never an asset to its owner and, even on its own, is usually a far greater liability to others than is generally realized. Packs (it needs only two to make a pack) of apparently harmless pet dogs—all let out to 'take themselves for a walk' every morning—have forced many farmers whose land adjoins suburban areas to give up keeping sheep.

In many 'civilized' dogs the sex instinct is far stronger than the hunting instinct, but not always in its true form. It may be perverted, and many dogs allowed to roam at will become canine 'homosexuals'. Such dogs are unlikely to get into the usual sort of dog trouble. They are, in fact, unlikely to have any of the characteristics of a *real* dog.

In training, the dog must be with you not merely in body; his mind must be with you too. It is easy to occupy the dog's mind from the start; to get it back once it has found ways of occupying itself is extremely difficult. To own a dog whose mind is always somewhere else is merely to own so much flesh and blood. In practically all dogs the sex instinct is almost certain to present itself as a distraction at some time or other, but in normal dogs it can be controlled by training. And in all dogs it can be removed or partially removed by the simple surgical operation of castration.

Like most other people I had always heard that castration completely ruined a dog's character but, unlike most other people, I do not believe all I hear. In horses it is general practice to castrate males not intended for breeding. Arkle, Foxhunter, Stroller and many others are names known to anyone remotely interested in horses—and they are all geldings. I had known neutred male cats which were terrific hunters with lots of character and intelligence, so why should dogs be so different?

In an effort to find out I wrote on the above lines in *Our Dogs* for which I was then (1950) a regular contributor. And I asked readers for their views. And I got them! Although forty letters is not all that many the views expressed (for *and* against) were so strong that I felt very satisfied with the result. So I wrote about the replies pointing out that of those I had received about 90 per cent were in favour. More important, all those in favour had owned castrated dogs while only one against had owned one and vowed never to have another. This brought more letters, some really nasty, accusing me of downright cruelty and saying that I was quite inhuman to even think of doing such a thing to a dog. But I still found that, by and large, those in favour had owned castrated dogs and those against had not. This strengthened my belief that the whole idea was due to ignorance and prejudice.

At that time many veterinary surgeons would refuse to castrate a dog because it was so 'harmful' (some still refuse) but I had just moved and my new vet was one who had castrated quite a number of dogs. (Incidentally most of the replies I had in favour of castration were from abroad.) So I tried to see some of those and was alarmed to find that, while some were all right, some were fat, horrible 'eunuchs'.

In those days I trained difficult and disobedient dogs belonging to other people and in some cases the sole cause of the trouble was that the dog was a sex maniac. Knowing that my vet would carry out the operation, I suggested to the owners that it might help to have the dog castrated. Anyone who has owned this type of dog will appreciate why the answer was always 'All right go ahead'. No matter how he changed, if there was any change at all it could not be for the worse!

As I said, these dogs were operated on by my own veterinary surgeon and then stayed with me for training. The changes which took place were nothing short of miraculous and, had I not seen it with my own eyes I would not have believed it possible. Horrible creatures were transformed into normal, likable animals during a period varying from two to six weeks.

Still I regarded this as a last resort operation. I had none of my own dogs castrated and did not recommend it except in the case of an over-sexed dog. Then one of my own Corgis developed an enlarged prostate gland which caused repeated stoppage of the bowel. My vet could only suggest castration or sloppy food, probably for the rest of his life. From the dog's point of view castration seemed the lesser of two evils and we had this done when he was six years old. Puck was not an over-sexed dog and the only change was in his health. This improved enormously due to his inside being able to function properly again. Naturally he lost interest in bitches but in no other way did he change *at all*.

Since then my knowledge of the subject—a most important

one to all pet dog owners—has increased to such an extent that I want to say a lot more about it than I did in the first edition of this book. Unfortunately for technical reasons outside my control, as the technicians would say, it is not possible to add several pages in the middle of a book which is already in print. I have, therefore, had to write an addendum which starts on page 189 to which I hope you will turn and read now.

THE INSTINCT TO BE CLEAN

Another instinct of importance is the instinct of the dog to keep its living quarters clean. This instinct is present in all animals born in nests (dogs, cats, pigs, etc.) as opposed to those born in the open, such as deer, horses or cattle. It is for this reason that it is virtually impossible to house-train a monkey while a pig presents no problem at all. As soon as they are old enough, cubs will leave the den to relieve themselves and will always go to the same place, usually some distance away. Given the opportunity, puppies will do the same.

If only people would remember that, much unnecessary cruelty could be avoided in the house-training of young puppies. It is also worth bearing in mind when choosing a puppy or an adult dog. Unfortunately, many are reared under conditions where they have no opportunity to be clean. In kennels that are too small, or are not cleaned out regularly and frequently, a puppy has no alternative to being dirty and will become accustomed to living in filthy conditions. Such a puppy is likely to be difficult to house-train, whereas one reared in a clean, roomy kennel will get into the habit of going as far as possible from its bed to relieve itself, and can usually be encouraged to go just a little bit farther (outside) when he goes to a new home.

Kennel-reared adults are likely to prove more difficult than puppies if they have been reared in kennels where dogs are left from about 5 p.m. until 8 a.m. Where this is done the kennel floors are usually sawdusted and the dogs get into the habit of doing what they want where and when they want to, a habit hard to break. In some kennels the dogs are encouraged to be clean—*not* by walloping poor little puppies with a folded newspaper for doing something Nature taught them to do the day they were born, or (even more horrible) by rubbing their noses in it, but simply by *allowing* them to be clean.

Our dogs are reared as kennel dogs, but we seldom have a puppy over six months old that fouls his kennel and some are quite clean much younger than that. We never take young puppies to sleep indoors but can take practically any of our adults to live indoors at any time, and I can, and often do, take a dog with me to stay in an hotel or with friends without any fear of 'mistakes'. Much of my time is spent travelling in a motor caravan and my wife and I have spent several nights in it accompanied by ten dogs. These dogs have had no 'house-training' whatever. They have simply been fed regularly, exercised regularly, including a walk at 7 a.m. and 9 p.m. *every* day, and have been given the opportunity to develop their natural instinct to be clean. If I sell a young dog that has taught himself to be clean he never presents any house-training problems to his new owner, on whom I impress the importance of sticking, as far as possible, to his regular routine, at least until he has settled down.

HOMING INSTINCT

Here we have an instinct which might not appear to be important in training, but it can, and should, be put to greater use. The homing instinct is common to many animals but, although most people marvel at the performances of homing pigeons (in which selective breeding has strengthened the ability to fly home hundreds of miles instinctively), few realize that a herd of cows which all walk into their own stalls do so in response to the same instinct.

It is for the same reason that a dog, given the opportunity, will adopt a basket, a chair or just a corner of the room as his 'home' and can be easily taught not to lie anywhere else. *Some* dogs will stay in a garden surrounded by a fence over which they could easily jump, and we had two Salukis which scaled high jumps of 10 ft. 6 in. and 10 ft. 3 in. living in a kennel with a run surrounded by a four-foot fence. Neither ever jumped out of his own 'home'.

CHAPTER V

INTELLIGENCE. SENSES. BALANCE OF INSTINCTS

INTELLIGENCE

Although intelligence is valued so much by dog owners, I doubt if any of the dog's other characteristics creates more misunderstanding. The wild dog used its intelligence not only to assist it in catching its prey, but also to evade capture by its enemies. Few owners appear to realize that the domestic dog also uses its intelligence for *two* purposes: (1) For the benefit of its master—to learn what he wants it to do. (2) For its own benefit—to find ways and means of evading the wishes of its master.

Whether intelligence is an asset to the owner or the dog depends largely on the owner (you cannot teach anyone who knows more than you do), but if it is an asset to the dog it is often a liability, sometimes a very big one, to the owner. Stupid dogs rarely become problem dogs. If we exclude bad temperaments, about which nothing can be done, practically all dogs sent to professional trainers as difficult are very intelligent. This intelligence the trainer finds most valuable in making the dog understand what he should do and that he *must* do it. However the dog, on returning home, finds it equally valuable in summing up the owner and saying to himself: 'This chap's a fool. I don't *have* to do it now so I won't!'

On the other hand, misunderstanding between man and dog can be due to the former overestimating the intelligence of the latter. This, combined with the idea that canine and human intelligence are the same, is probably the cause of more failures in training than any other factor. Many dogs are punished by owners who believe that 'He knows what I want him to do' when the dog has no idea. These dogs are often punished for trying their very hardest to please an owner who cannot make himself understood. Such owners, by believing their dogs are more intelligent than they really are, usually cause

E 65

great mental distress in their dogs—a common, if unintentional, form of cruelty.

Wisely used, intelligence is one of the greatest assets in training. I have known dogs with a very strong submissive instinct that would do anything to please, but so 'dim' that it was almost impossible to make them understand what was wanted. Many of my best dogs, on the other hand, have had limited submissive instinct but abundant intelligence. They had little desire to please me but, because of their intelligence, it was possible to make them understand that it was to their *own* advantage to do so. One has to be firm with such dogs until they have realized that doing what they want to do has unpleasant consequences. After that the submissive instinct begins to develop and the task becomes progressively easier.

Intelligence shows itself much earlier than temperament or most of the instincts. By studying a litter, one can often pick out, as early as three or four weeks, a puppy that is 'quicker in the uptake' than his brothers and sisters. It does not follow that he will be easy to train, but when trained he stands a good chance of being the best of the litter. These bright puppies are usually mischievous and wilful (leaders rather than followers) and, unless their owner is capable of using this intelligence to his advantage, they will certainly use it to their own.

Although intelligence shows at an earlier age than temperament, the best guide as to how a young puppy will finish up is still to be found in the parents and other relatives. Some guidance can, however, be obtained from the appearance of the animal itself.

A bright eye usually denotes a bright dog, but be careful not to confuse intelligence and temperament. The dog possessing a shifty, furtive eye may have exceptional intelligence and so may one with a mean, piggy expression. Either could often be more accurately described as cunning.

Shape of head, too, would appear to have some bearing on intelligence. I like a good wide skull with a well-defined stop (where skull joins foreface). From that I do not wish to imply that the wider the skull the more intelligent the dog. As in everything connected with livestock, extremes should always be avoided. Size does not seem to matter, and distance between ears is governed by their position on the skull, not by its width.

Distance between the eyes is important but don't forget what I have already said in connection with temperament. Length of skull from the bump on the top (the occiput) to the stop is as important as width. The type of head I like is a little longer than it is broad, a little narrower at the eyes than at the ears, but I prefer a square skull to one that is too long. The foreface and muzzle seem to have no connection with mentality, as one finds intelligent working dogs with fairly long and fairly short forefaces.

There are many who disagree on this subject, and a head of the shape I have in mind would be regarded as a serious fault in some show breeds. In spite of the many arguments I have heard against it, I still believe that I am right and have several reasons for this belief. Firstly, of the hundreds of dogs I have had in my care, the most intelligent have possessed skulls of the shape described. Secondly, all the shepherds, gamekeepers, poachers, ratcatchers, huntsmen and other working-dog men I have known prefer that shape. Dogs are part of the lives of these men, whose knowledge has often been handed down from generation to generation, and I cannot believe that they are all wrong. Thirdly, and perhaps most important of all, is the fact that *all* wild dogs, all dogs which have reverted to nature (the out-and-out mongrels), and practically all working dogs have skulls of similar shape.

Only in some show breeds do we find any great deviation, and my experience is that the further one deviates from what I regard as a normal head, the less likelihood there seems to be of finding intelligence. Although they may appear very different, there is fundamentally very little difference in the shape of skull of *working* breeds throughout the world. The heavy lips on some breeds alter the outward appearance of the head, as do ears and coat. Few people would at first glance regard the Spaniel (working type), with its long, pendulous ears, as having a head of similar shape to that of the Alsatian with its prick ears, but on close examination it will be found to be not so very different.

THE SENSES

The dog, like us, has five senses, four of which are important in training, but their strength differs very considerably from our own.

Smell. By far the most important to mankind is the sense of smell, and here the dog leaves us so far behind that even scientists are still not sure what 'scent' really is. 'Nose', as it is called, varies considerably between breeds and individuals, but it is wrong to assume that because dogs like Greyhounds or Salukis prefer to hunt by sight they cannot use their noses.

Hearing. Next in usefulness is the sense of hearing, also much more powerful than our own. Not only can the dog hear a sound which no human ear could pick up; it can also differentiate between similar sounds much more accurately than we can. Although, for instance, I may be unable to decide whether my wife is calling 'Pip' or 'Gyp', neither of these bitches will answer to the other's name, and a dog rarely has difficulty in recognizing its master's footstep amongst a lot of others, or the sound of its 'own' motor-car.

Sight. Though there is some difference of opinion, it is generally believed that the dog sees only in black and white. This is possibly correct, but I disagree with those who maintain that his sight is in any other way inferior to our own. A person often has the advantage that he or she can see over obstacles which may block the dog's view, but many dogs can spot a hare or a rabbit at a distance at which it is imperceptible to the human eye.

Important in training is the fact that a dog's powers of observation are far keener than those of the average human. It will note a slight movement of the body, a flick of the finger, or even a wink of the eye, which would pass unnoticed by most people. Combined with the dog's quick mental reactions, this often makes people believe that their dog 'understands every word', whereas, in fact, he *sees* some signal which they did not expect him to notice. It also makes it possible for highly trained dogs to appear capable of doing arithmetic and other things which dogs *cannot* do. These dogs are, in fact, reacting to signals imperceptible to a human audience. Many highly trained, sensitive dogs will react to changes in their trainer's expression. So much so that it is almost impossible to draw a line between power of observation and mind-reading. The percentage of such dogs is so small, and the number of owners with the sort of mind a dog can understand even smaller, that this special power is rarely of importance in the training of the family dog.

Touch. The sense of touch varies tremendously between different dogs, due chiefly to the amount of 'clothing' the dog wears. Many people forget this and will slap a puppy (which they should never do, anyhow) that has a fine coat just as hard as one with a thick, woolly coat. Not only does coat texture make a difference; we have thick-skinned and thin-skinned dogs. For instance, if you take the loose skin of a Greyhound between the finger and thumb, it feels like thin velvet, but if you try to do the same with a Terrier it feels more like thick leather. What would cause very severe pain to the one would not be felt *at all* by the other.

Another mistake is to compare the dog's sense of touch with our own. I have heard it argued that a dog's neck and throat are as sensitive as a human's and that it is, therefore, cruel to jerk it with a chain collar. To realize how fantastic such an idea is, one has only to watch puppies at play. They will 'worry' each other by the throat, two or three often tugging at one in opposite directions. Only occasionally does this appear to hurt the victim. If, however, one lets a little puppy, or worse still puppies, 'worry' one's hand, one is left in no doubt as to the amount of pain their needle-sharp teeth are capable of inflicting! To imagine them hanging on to one's throat shows how impossible it is to compare our sense of touch with a dog's.

Balance

So far, we have dealt with the characteristics, good and bad, with which the dog is born, but two dogs born with identical mental make-up (I do not think that has ever happened) might finish up entirely different animals. They would both retain inherent characteristics, but the extent and direction of development would depend on two things: (a) how these characteristics balance each other and (b) the dog's upbringing. In other words, a great deal depends on the owner to see that desirable characteristics are developed sufficiently to counter-balance undesirable ones, and not *vice versa* as all too often happens.

We might compare a dog with an herbaceous border, the effect of which depends on a combination of factors, the most important of which are plants, soil, and the skill of the gardener. It is possible to select a mixture of plants which, under suitable soil conditions, will not only compete against each other (so that none will get out of control) but will form a growth of such luxuriance that it is almost impossible for weeds to grow at all. To the keen gardener, however, that is a lazy idea and he plants the plants he likes, relying on his skill and energy either to encourage them to grow or to keep them from getting out of hand. It must never be forgotten that some of the most beautiful flowers, when left to Nature, can become most obnoxious weeds.

To satisfy his desire for a dog that will *do* something, the keen dog trainer, like the keen gardener, is prepared to accept certain factors, though knowing that he will have to devote much skill and energy to keeping them under control. Few dog owners, however, are keen or skilled trainers, and most want something that will give maximum pleasure with minimum trouble. Unlike gardeners, the prospective dog owner cannot buy a mixture of separate factors likely to suit his particular conditions. He must buy an animal in which those factors may be present or absent, and if present, they cannot be seen. In a puppy they may not have started to develop but they may be there, and one cannot tell how strong they will be when they have developed. The result is that many people who, like a lazy gardener, want something that will more or less keep itself under control, end up with a dog which, without serious training, becomes a liability.

Some dogs do turn up with all the essential factors so nearly balanced that little training is necessary, but, unfortunately, they are few and far between. In choosing a dog it is always worth going to a great deal of trouble to try to find one with normal instincts and a good temperament. Instinct makes a dog do something in response to an urge, initiative makes him want to do it, intelligence enables him to do it well, but it is *your* dog's temperament that decides how *you* should teach him what you want him to do. The genius, either canine or human, is often highly strung and temperamental; the best friend in time of need is usually the placid sort with 'his head screwed on the right way'.

While on that note I must refer to the importance of the

balance of the mind itself. Insanity in dogs is far more prevalent than most people imagine and appears to me to be on the increase. This may be due to many causes. There are active-minded dogs cooped up until they go mad; there is the hyper-sensitive type in a house full of rowdy children or with a bad-tempered owner.

These are only two examples of acquired insanity, which will sometimes depart with a complete change of environment —and which will not occur at all if you take the trouble to acquire some dog-sense. What may affect you is hereditary insanity, which renders a dog useless for any purpose. Usually this weakness can be detected in quite young puppies. It is difficult to explain how; they just look 'away' with a sort of glassy eye and they do not play normal puppy games. Often they have some sort of obsession, such as 'eating' water instead of drinking. It is very obvious in the adult, but I can describe it only by saying that the sufferer 'looks barmy'.

Disease, particularly Hard Pad or Distemper, often affects the brain. This may only be temporary and an almost complete recovery is sometimes made. Unfortunately, however, from the considerable experience of Hard Pad I had before much was known about it, I found that dogs which had shown nervous symptoms never became *quite* the same mentally as they were before. That type of nervous disorder is not, of course, hereditary and there is no reason why the puppies from parents affected in this way should not be perfectly normal. The danger lies in the fact that, if one has a dog that is a bit 'peculiar', one is apt, if it has had Hard Pad, to blame that disease. What one cannot be sure of is that it would not have turned 'peculiar' anyhow, owing to the trouble being hereditary.

CHAPTER VI

FINDING THE RIGHT DOG

Pedigree or Mongrel—What breed?—Suitability for children—Puppy or
adult—Dog shows—Responsibilities of ownership

We now come to the problem of how to tell whether a dog is
likely to possess as many as possible of the factors you want and
as few as possible of those you don't want. What makes this an
even greater problem than it would otherwise be is the fact that
most people buy a puppy at an age before most of the factors
have started to develop.

The best guide, therefore, and in many cases the only guide,
lies in the puppy's pedigree. Unfortunately, in dogs, the word
is usually something associated with shows and, although of
considerable 'snob value' to many owners, there are few to
whom it is of any real value. The value of pedigree in the
breeding of show dogs is generally realized but it is not so well
known that in the breeding of working dogs it is of even greater
importance. It is possible for a good judge to tell whether a dog
will win prizes simply by looking at it, but the only guides to
working ability are actual tests or the study of a dog's pedigree.

The Greyhound is a good example of the relative value of
pedigree in a show or working dog, as the Greyhound Stud
Book is what is known as a 'closed book'. That, in effect, means
that a dog, even if its pedigree is known, cannot be registered
unless both its parents were registered, which also means that
none of that dog's descendants can ever be registered. As only
registered dogs can be entered in recognized races or coursing
matches, a Greyhound 'without papers' is of little or no value
as a worker. Any dog, however, so long as it looks like the breed
it is supposed to be, may be registered at the Kennel Club and
there is no reason why a dog of unknown pedigree should not
win Best in Show at Cruft's.

There is no reason, either, why such a dog should not be
a good worker, but one cannot tell by just looking at it what sort

of worker a dog is. Neither is there any reason why such a dog should not be an excellent companion and guard, but the only guide as to whether a puppy will grow up to be one lies in its pedigree.

This raises the question of what *is* a pedigree, and what is its value? To most owners, and to many breeders, it is simply a piece of paper with a lot of names on it, worth exactly what a piece of paper is worth. To the experienced breeder, however, it could be described as a picture of a lot of animals—of inestimable value in breeding operations. The fact is often overlooked that *every* dog has a pedigree, some carefully and authentically kept for generations, some 'manufactured' by unscrupulous breeders and dealers and some which have never been recorded. A pedigree does not make a dog good or bad; it is merely a guide as to what a puppy is likely to become, and as to the sort of puppies, good *or* bad, a particular bitch is likely to produce when mated to a certain dog.

A pedigree is of no real value to anyone who does not know, 'personally' or by repute, the dogs and bitches whose names appear on that piece of paper. As it is unlikely that you will know many of the dogs whose names appear, even if you do understand how to read the pedigree, you will have to rely on the advice of someone who does. The difficulty in seeking this advice lies in the fact that, although there are many who can tell you what all, or nearly all, the dogs in a pedigree *looked* like and what prizes they have won, there are few who can tell you what they were like *as dogs*. I am not suggesting that good looks are of no importance except in the show ring, as, although the initial cost may be slightly greater, the upkeep of a good looker that will be a continual source of admiration is no greater than that of a nondescript. But the greatest pleasures in owning a dog arise, not from what it *looks like*, but from what *it is*, and unless your adviser knows something of the characters of the dogs in a pedigree his or her advice will be worth just as little as the pedigree itself.

Many people imagine that length of pedigree is the all-important factor. Actually, the length of a pedigree depends chiefly on the number of names a breeder feels inclined to write out. I have had Corgis, my own breeding in an unbroken line for ten generations on one side and eleven on the other, for which I could, with hardly any reference to records, have written out an eleven-generation pedigree. The reason I did not was because it would have meant writing out 4,094 names!

Now for a few words about in-breeding and line-breeding, the latter being, as far as we are concerned, just a mild version of the former. Many people, when they talk about a dog being 'highly bred', have a hazy idea of in-breeding, which in many quarters is regarded as the root of all evils in animals—a view, unfortunately, held by many who should know better.

In-breeding produces nothing; it merely accentuates or concentrates that which is already there. If a half-brother and sister are mated and produce nervous puppies it is not because the parents were related but because the common grandparent was either nervous, or carried the blood of a high percentage of nervous ancestors. These puppies, being in-bred, would be more likely to transmit nervousness to their progeny than if the parents had been unrelated. But, had the common grandparent had a firm, bold temperament, a good constitution, and had it been descended from stock with these qualities, the same thing would have happened in reverse.

Temperament can be *improved* by in-breeding, just as it can be ruined, although I must admit that, in show dogs, the latter has happened more often than the former. That is due to the fact that most breeders, in their fanatical efforts to produce Champions, in-breed for certain physical qualities, at the same time in-breeding for bad temperament. If, for instance, long heads are fashionable in a particular breed and a certain dog, Champion Long Face, has a longer head than all other Champions, breeders from far and near will send bitches to be mated to him. It is probable that many of the puppies so produced will have longer heads than their dams, and it is equally probable that many of the bitch puppies will in turn be mated back to their sire. The progeny of these matings would almost certainly show a 'great improvement' so far as length of head is concerned—all very well if you regard as improvement the production of heads that are caricatures.

Whether the improvement is real or imaginary does not really matter. What matters is that if Champion Long Face is mentally deficient he will produce a great many children, and even more grandchildren, that 'excel in length of head', but which are also mentally deficient, probably to a greater extent than their grandsire.

That, however, should not happen, and if a certain name recurs several times on both sides of the pedigree of a puppy, do not jump to the conclusion that it will inevitably be nervous and delicate. If the dog possessing the recurring name had the slightest tendency to be nervous or delicate, or if he was descended from stock with those tendencies, there is every chance that they will show in the puppy. If, however, this dog was bold, had a robust constitution and was bred from stock possessing the same qualities, the chances of the puppy growing into a bold, robust dog are *far* greater than if it were the result of mating entirely unrelated parents.

To me, a nervous or delicate dog is useless and, although I regard good looks as very desirable, good temperaments and robust constitutions are absolutely essential. In trying to get such dogs I carefully line-breed to dogs possessing these essentials in good measure; in other words, I in-breed to dogs possessing the qualities I hope to obtain in the puppies. In Corgis I continued this practice for well over 20 years with no regrets whatsoever. Two of the toughest dogs of any breed that I have ever owned were Jix and Pip, litter brother and sister, produced by mating two full cousins which were bred from related stock for several generations further back.

Here, again, an idea prevails that in-breeding is something connected only with show dogs. But if the pedigrees of all dogs at the International Sheepdog Trials were studied it would probably be found that more in-breeding is practised than in the case of the dogs at Cruft's Dog Show. All breeds of livestock have been produced by in-breeding and/or line-breeding, and could not have been produced otherwise.

Many people maintain that mongrels are more intelligent, and have more character, than pedigree dogs. Many of these people, however, 'prove' their argument by comparing a particularly intelligent mongrel with an equally stupid pedigree dog, just as some people compare two breeds by contrasting a stupid individual of one with an intelligent individual of another. All that is proved by such a comparison is the stupidity of those who make it. If mongrels are superior it seems strange that they are never used by shepherds, gamekeepers, or the Police Forces.

It should be noticed that a cross-bred is *not* a mongrel, neither is any dog necessarily a mongrel because it does not happen to have a known pedigree. One of our purest native breeds, the Working Collie, is bred by men who rarely bother to write out pedigrees, but, because they only breed from the best workers, this breed carries less foreign blood than the vast majority of pedigree show dogs.

To me, a real mongrel is a dog descended from generations of mongrels, with every now and again a dash of pure blood thrown in. They are not bred—they just happen! In many cases they are exceptionally intelligent, but often they use their intelligence only to suit their own purposes. Such dogs have little or no submissive instinct; their whole outlook is centred on themselves, on having a good time in the way or ways they fancy—which rarely appeal to dog owners! These characteristics are sometimes due to environment, as most of the people who let their dogs out, instead of taking them out, keep mongrels. Usually, however, they are hereditary, for reasons already explained when discussing the sex instinct.

From that it must not be concluded that all mongrels are undesirable. I have come across many, sensibly brought up, that were really nice dogs. In choosing a dog, I know no better way of buying a 'pig in a poke' than to get a mongrel puppy. Some people like to take a chance but, if you are not that sort, I advise you to buy a puppy of a pure breed which will at least have a reasonable opportunity of turning out something like its parents. On the other hand, if you are offered an adult dog that is being disposed of *for some good reason*, do not turn it down simply because it is a mongrel. By that time you can form an opinion of the dog itself and so long as *he* is all right parentage matters not.

Which brings us to the question of *what breed should you have?* The Kennel Club recognizes nearly 130 breeds and varieties and as there are many which are not yet recognized I should think there must be well over 250 pure breeds of dog in the world. You will see, therefore, how impossible it is to compare them all, but there are some points worth noting when deciding which to have.

When people ask me which is the most intelligent breed, I invariably reply that there is no such thing. There are intelligent and stupid dogs, courageous and cowardly ones, hard and soft, and, to sum up, good, bad and indifferent dogs in *every* breed.

It does not follow, however, that the breed is of no importance, as some produce a high percentage of good dogs while others produce an even higher percentage of bad ones. It should be noted, too, that what is a good dog to one person may be an equally bad one to another. My advice is: (*a*) sort out several breeds that will suit your purpose; (*b*) from these select one or two you like; (*c*) try to find a suitable *individual* of that breed that is likely to suit *you*.

There are, of course, books on all the more popular breeds, but many of these can be compared to seedsmen's catalogues. There is no harm hoping that the seeds you buy may grow into flowers like those so beautifully portrayed, but if you depend on each and every seed growing into a flower of such beauty, you are almost certainly doomed to disappointment. Apart from information on show points, these books, read intelligently, often help to give some idea of the type of work for which the breed was originally used. This helps in forming an impression of the mental characteristics to expect—especially of the instincts that are likely to be strongest.

Breed is a matter of personal taste, but if you want a healthy dog that can be easily trained I must advise you never to go to extremes. If you like a small or a big dog, have one, but don't search for the *smallest* or the *biggest*. You can also have a dog with short legs or a long coat without having one with the *shortest* legs or *longest* coat.

More important than the breed itself is the particular strain of that breed. Some breeders regard as essential certain characteristics to which others pay little attention. These are usually physical properties which can be seen in the show ring, but some breeders do pay the very greatest attention to character, and in particular to temperament. Consequently, we find in breeds reputed to be snappy and bad-tempered, strains that are quite the reverse; in breeds supposed to be suspicious of strangers (many of which are afraid of them), strains that are bold and friendly; in breeds that are supposed to fight, strains that have little inclination to do so. Don't forget, however, that this works the other way too. In breeds reputed to be guards there are strains that would run a mile from a burglar, while there are, in breeds reputed to be good-tempered, reliable with children or even sloppy, strains that are thoroughly unreliable or even dangerous.

A strain is not a lot of dogs owned by one person and all bearing the same prefix or affix. It could be described as a big family all having certain characteristics in common, and the closer the relationship the more likely is a puppy from that strain to develop these characteristics—*good or bad*.

Much thought is usually given to the question of size, often based on the belief that living in a small house means keeping a small dog. There are also people who would like a dog but wonder whether it would be fair to keep one (especially a big one) in a town.

Whether the dog will have a good or a bad home, whether it should be a big or small dog, depends, not on where you live, but on *you*. Whether you live in a mansion in the country or in a London tenement matters not the slightest. What matters is whether or not you are prepared to accept the responsibility of owning a dog. Far too many people think that they carry out that responsibility if they see that their dog is well fed and has a comfortable bed, but overlook the questions of exercising and seeing to the dog's mental as well as its physical well-being.

The amount of exercise a dog requires varies very considerably between different breeds and different ages, and also between individual dogs of the same breed and age. Exercise and training can be co-ordinated with advantage. A boisterous young dog will be much easier to train if he has plenty of exercise. Many young dogs which get into trouble do so as a direct result of too little exercise.

On the other hand, many unfortunate puppies are dragged out for 'walks' which are far beyond their strength. Up to four or five months any puppy will get adequate exercise in a garden, although, for the sake of the garden, it may be advisable to find some other place if you own a big breed. No dog will play on its own for any length of time and, having taken a puppy from its brothers and sisters with whom it would play, it is up to you to replace them by playing with it yourself.

To walk a dog to the end of the street and back on a lead is not exercise. Anyone with any consideration will see that his dog is allowed to run free in some place where he can gallop and stretch himself and where there is no risk of traffic. One good daily walk will suffice, but if a dog is expected to be clean in the house he should be allowed out to relieve himself (not on the street) at least twice again. A little common sense helps in deciding how much exercise is necessary. Speaking generally, big dogs require more than small ones, and they require much more room in which to take it.

A big dog is no more difficult to train than a little one, sometimes easier, but an untrained big dog is obviously a bigger handful than an untrained little one. Size would appear to have no connection with intelligence and, provided they are physically capable, little dogs can be taught to do anything that a big one can do. If you want a dog for protection, a fairly big one is more likely to deter wrongdoers than a little one, but a little one with plenty of spirit is more useful than some of the shivering, cowardly brutes I have seen that have been bought as guards.

The common question 'Are they good with children?' can often be answered by asking 'Are the children good with dogs?' All dogs with temperaments already described as good (free from nervousness or bad temper) are not suitable as pets for children. Many of them are far too high-spirited and, if played with by children, will almost certainly become rowdy. Many dogs that bite children do so through no evil intentions whatsoever. They do it merely through the hunting instinct prompting them to grab something running away; and a child makes just as good a 'bite' as anything else. Sensible dogs do not do that, and it is nothing short of astounding how sensible some dogs can be under the most trying circumstances. Many dogs, however, without being nervous or bad-tempered, are so high-spirited that, when they get a bit excited, they do things which, I am sure, are quite unintentional—usually barking incessantly, and/or biting. Of all the incentives likely to get an excitable dog worked up I know of nothing to equal a crowd of children, and many of the best dogs (for those who want to train them to do something) are quite unsuitable for children. Most dogs brought up with children become very fond of them, they enjoy entering into the same games and resemble the children in many ways.

Most children like a little puppy, which is all right if they can be made to understand that a puppy is not a toy but a baby that requires just as much care and consideration as they did. For toddlers I think it is very unkind to get a little puppy. It nearly always presents a 'two-way' problem. A puppy and a child will play with each other as readily as with playmates of their own species. They have, however, very different ideas of fun; the child's podgy hands are no match for a puppy's sharp milk teeth and most of the games end up in tears. The child is too young to understand why the puppy should bite and the puppy is too young to understand why it should not.

The ideal for a child is a steady adult dog used to children, but, as that is often difficult to obtain, you may have to look for a puppy about six months old. A dog with a very placid temperament, even a downright lazy one, is always the best for children. Such dogs are often extremely intelligent and staunch guards but they just don't believe in tearing about for nothing. Playing with children helps to prevent their becoming over-fat and lethargic, as often otherwise happens.

There is, of course, a common belief that a dog will not become attached to anyone unless obtained young—when not more than about eight weeks old. If people would only think for a minute they would realize what a ridiculous idea that is. The Police, the Army, the R.A.F., the Guide Dogs for the Blind organization and most trainers will not accept a dog under a year old. The majority of these dogs, trained to a standard far above average, develop an affection for their handlers greater than that ever experienced by the average pet owner.

Most dogs which came to me for corrective training were between one and two years old and had nearly always lived with their owners since they were small puppies. We usually kept these dogs four to six weeks, and at the end of that time many showed more affection for us than ever they did for their owners.

We never buy a young puppy if we can help it. Round about a year is a nice age but many of the best dogs we have owned have been much older than that—and often completely out of hand—when acquired by us. Sometimes we want to retire a dog which we feel would be happier in a private home than as a member of a pack. We always try to put the dog's happiness before our own and if we can find a suitable home we have no qualms about giving away such a dog. Many have lived happily ever after and given years of pleasure to their new owners. Many people believe that their dog could not live without them simply because that is what they want to believe. From experience of boarding many hundreds of dogs I know that only a tiny minority ever fret for their owners. The majority seem only too pleased to get away from them and the more fuss the owner makes the more relieved does the dog appear to be!

Of course an adult dog does not always settle down in a new home, but if it does not, the chances are that that particular dog in that particular home would not have been a success anyhow.

I am not advising you to go looking for an old dog (it is highly unlikely that you will find one, anyhow), but do not turn down a suitable adult because you think it is too old to become attached to you. There are quite a number of arguments for and against both adult and puppy. The selection of puppies offered for sale is much higher than that of adults. Under favourable conditions a puppy can go to a new home after it is six weeks old (I prefer to keep mine another fortnight) but at that age it is almost impossible to form anything like an accurate picture of what the puppy will grow up to be. In an adult, however, you can see what the dog is.

Be sure to find out why an adult dog is for sale. Quite often people ring me up to ask if I know anyone wanting a young dog. When I ask why the owners want to get rid of him the answer is often on the lines of: 'Well, as a matter of fact, he bit the postman this morning, and he doesn't like being moved out of his chair and he bit my little boy—oh, not very badly— when he tried to move him. He's really a dear, so affectionate with people he knows—so long as they leave him alone. We're really terribly fond of him and, of course, he must go to a good home—we would not just let him go to anybody.' As if anybody would want to have him!

The reason why quite a number of dogs, particularly young

F

ones, are offered for sale is that they have developed some bad habit or habits. On the other hand, people do sometimes have to get rid of a perfectly good dog for domestic reasons, posting abroad of servicemen being a common example, and, because of this ridiculous idea about adult dogs not taking to new homes, they often have difficulty in giving them away, far less selling them.

Breeders, too, often 'run on' one or two puppies in the hope that they will be up to show standard, but their hopes are not always realized so that often these puppies are offered for sale at six to twelve months old. By then they are over teething, are usually inoculated and the price asked is not usually much more than that which would have been asked for the same dog at eight weeks. It is often possible to buy a young dog for less than the cost of the food he has eaten.

Great care should be taken in choosing an adult dog for children, as a dog's reaction to a child and a grown-up may be quite different. My experience is that dogs either like or dislike children, rarely tolerating them as they often will adults. When I sell or give away a dog I insist that, if it proves unsuitable, I shall have it back. I have known dogs that would not settle down in a home which in every way appeared perfect, but on going to another home have settled down right away. Moreover, the first people might get another dog that would be a great success; which brings us back to the importance of a dog that suits *you*. For the dog's sake and your own, therefore, I advise having it on approval, unless it is a young puppy, when, owing to the risk of disease, few breeders will agree to that.

Having made several references to show and working dogs, I feel that I should, perhaps, say something about dog shows. These were started in 1859, no doubt by owners who took a pride in the appearance of their working dogs and who thought that it might be a good idea to hold meetings to decide whose were the best looking. So popular did this 'dog game' become, that, in a short time, a dog that could win in the show ring might be of greater value than a good worker. In other words, for the first time in history, a dog that could do nothing, which had hitherto been regarded as useless, could be worth more money than one which would work.

Few people realize the tremendous effect that one fact has had on the present-day dog population. In practically every breed that is still worked there are now two types, the working and the show type. In many cases the types differ so much that they are, to all intents and purposes, distinct breeds. We also find two types of breeder: one concentrating on work only, often running his dogs in trials that suit his particular breed; the other, the dyed-in-the-wool exhibitor who values a dog only as a potential winner of prizes in the show ring.

Man tamed the wild dog and from it bred a wonderful collection of useful working breeds. Since shows started, however, the popularity of the dog has increased beyond all expectation and the majority are now kept by a very different type of owner, and under very different conditions, than in days of old. Modern man has not, however, followed the example of his forefathers and bred dogs suitable for these conditions. Instead, he has, in many cases, taken those wonderful working breeds and, from them, produced an assortment of freaks the like of which have never been seen in any other class of livestock. That, I may say, is a view held by the vast majority of people who work and train dogs, and it has, on more than one occasion, been expressed in public by eminent veterinary surgeons.

Fortunately, all breeds have not been turned into caricatures in this way and there *are* good working dogs that can win, and have won, top awards in the show ring. It must be admitted, however, that the percentage is small. One of the most successful men in the dog game wins prizes both at shows and in field trials with the same breed. But he does it with different strains which, as I have already mentioned, are really of two different breeds, one bred for trials, the other for shows. The two are never crossed and differ in appearance and in many other ways. Plate III illustrates two of the many examples of the changes that have taken place in the appearance of some show breeds.

No-one can claim that any breed, as a breed, has had its working ability improved as a result of dog shows. To anyone who has ever worked a dog, it is obviously a physical impossibility for some of our show-ring winners to do the work for which they were originally intended. So far as you are concerned, however, many show breeds *have* improved and it is from one or other of the show strains that you are more likely to find a good pet than from a strain bred *solely* for work.

The reason is that, in strains bred for show, some of which have not had any opportunity to work for generations, the instinct to do so has become weaker. It is the instinct to work, however, that gets pet dogs into trouble.

The reason the working instinct is weaker in show strains is not, as might at first appear, due to the fact that a dog bred from trained parents will be more easily trained than one bred from untrained parents. Quite the reverse can be, and often is, the case. To breed dogs for work the policy should not be to breed from dogs that can be trained to work but from dogs that will work with a minimum of training. As one who has spent a lifetime among working dogs, I can assure you that there is all the difference between the two, but many dogs, particularly show dogs, that *would* have worked with a minimum of training have never had a chance to do so. Those dogs are far more likely to produce progeny that will work than dogs that have been trained by a skilled trainer—perhaps with some considerable difficulty.

I am convinced, however, that many show dogs would not, in many cases could not, work, no matter how clever the trainer who took them in hand. That they appear capable of working may be true, but they have been born with the instinct to work very weak, or even completely lacking, and no one can tell, by looking at a lot of dogs which will work with a minimum of training, which can be encouraged to work in some sort of way and which will not work at all. As dogs from show strains rarely have the opportunity to prove whether they can or will work, no one knows which sort they are breeding from, but it is safe to say that in *all* show breeds there are winning dogs which have no inclination to work. Every time one of these dogs is bred from, the average strength of the working instinct throughout the breed is diluted. As I hope you will have realized by now, instincts rarely, if ever, die, even when not used for generations, and the majority of show breeds have the instinct for which they were originally bred present in some degree. The strength is invariably weaker, however, in the show strains than in the strains bred for work; in other

PLATE V

If you don't move towards the puppy he will eventually move towards you

PLATE VI

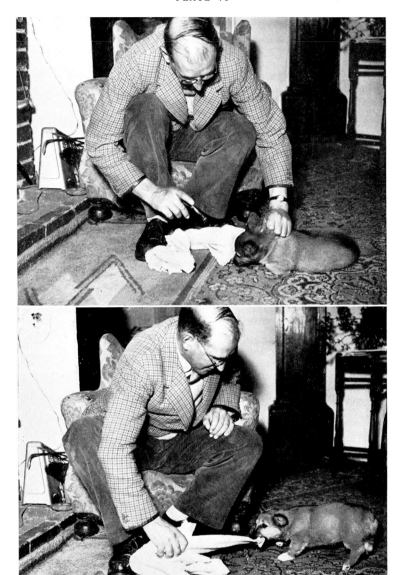

RIGHT AND WRONG
(a) Teaching a puppy to let go
(b) Unintentionally teaching him to hang on

words, the average show dog has much less desire to work than the average dog from a working strain. Note that I say 'average', as it is possible to find an individual show dog with a much stronger working instinct than one from a working strain.

Although very sad to those who like to work dogs, the fact that the modern show dog has less desire to work than his working ancestors is of the greatest benefit to you. It must not be forgotten, however, that the lack of desire to follow an instinct may not be due entirely to weakness in the instinct itself. Very often it is due to lack of initiative, usually accompanied by a general weakness in character. Some breeds have undoubtedly lost much of their character by breeding for *exaggerated* show points, but, fortunately, this does not apply to all breeds, or even to all dogs of a particular breed.

Never have I known two dogs with more character than Nippy of Drumharrow and International Champion Formakin Orangeman. Nippy was my first Corgi, the best cattle dog and ratter I ever knew, and she won a Challenge Certificate and two reserve C.C.s as long ago as 1936. Many a time I had her working with cattle till evening, cleaned the mud off her, put her on the night train from Perth to travel to Euston, where she was met in the morning, to be shown by a complete stranger and returned that night from London ready for her work next morning. So keen did she become on these outings that, if she saw an open travelling box, she would get in, hoping to be sent off. Paddy, as he was known at home, was both a great grandson and a great-great-great-grandson of Nippy. At the first twelve Championship Shows held after the war he won eight Challenge Certificates (five of them in succession) and two reserve C.C.s. He was the first Corgi to win Best in Show at a Championship Show and, after I exported him at a record price, he quickly became an American and a Canadian Champion. His great character also won for him as many admirers on the other side of the Atlantic as it had done on this.

Although it is impossible, without an actual test, to tell whether or not a dog has the instinct to work, it is possible to form some idea of its character by simply studying it carefully. One has really to know a dog to assess its character accurately, but a fairly accurate impression can be formed by careful observation.

Returning to dog shows themselves, I think they can be of value to the pet dog owner as well as to the breeder and I strongly advise anyone thinking of buying a dog to attend several. Shows form quite the best means of seeing what the various breeds look like.

Of greater importance is the fact that, by watching the dogs being judged, you will be able to form some idea of the characteristics of the various breeds, as breeds. If, for instance, most of the dogs of one breed are cringing and trying to hide behind their owners my advice is to move on to another. If you have your mind set on that breed you may be able to find an individual with a good temperament, and you should note by means of your catalogue how the dogs with good temperaments are bred and try to get a puppy from that strain. Even then the risk is far greater than if you choose a puppy from a breed in which bad temperaments are the exception rather than the rule.

The same applies to fighting, and if you see a ring full of dogs screaming and yelling to get at each others' throats, a not uncommon sight, you can expect a puppy, especially a dog puppy, of that breed to have a strong tendency to fight. If, on the other hand, all the dogs of a particular breed seem to be sensible and non-aggressive, then the risk of a puppy of that breed turning out to be a fighter will be much less.

It is sometimes said that a dog that is a good 'shower', must have a good temperament, but that is only true to a certain extent. A submissive dog will respond to the voice of its master, a greedy dog will respond to food—both will cock their ears, wag their tails and look alive and alert. Any dog, however, that gets all excited, tail a-quiver, eyes nearly popping out of its head, *at nothing*, is mad, and if you watch some of the big winners in certain breeds you will see that is what they do.

Apart from watching the dogs in the ring, you can learn a great deal by quietly watching them on their benches—not by 'loving' them all and spreading disease from one to the other, but just by careful observation. You will notice that with some breeds practically all the dogs spend their entire day yapping and barking, while with others the majority just curl up and go to sleep. If you want a dog that is continually yapping at nothing, then you might have one of the former, but if you want a nice quiet sensible dog about the place, then I strongly advise you to choose one of the latter. You don't want a dog that just curls up and goes to sleep? Neither do I, but if you had gone to a show where my dogs were entered you would have found them all (except perhaps youngsters) lying quietly on their benches. After a dog has been to one or two shows there is nothing to get excited about, and most sensible dogs find them rather boring. Dogs that get excited over nothing are usually a nuisance and likely to get on most people's nerves.

At shows you are likely to see obedience competitions, the first real effort to provide the dog, whose owner cannot provide it with any work, with something to do. These competitions are not generally favoured, and indeed often ridiculed, by working-dog owners. Used as a means to an end—a more obedient dog —the standard obedience exercises can be of great value. Unfortunately, they are too often regarded as an end in themselves—a means of winning prizes—and the extremes to which some training enthusiasts will go to win these prizes are no less than the extremes to which dogs have been bred to win in the show ring. Often they kill much of the dog's initiative and individuality, turning him into something which answers implicitly each command or signal but which would never dream of doing anything on its own.

Unfortunately, these competitions are at present of little help in the breeding of trainable dogs. They show what a dog can be taught to do but give no indication as to the amount of trouble and skill that has been involved in getting him to do it. Unless the exercises become more practical, these competitions will test the skill of the trainer to a *far* greater extent than the trainability of the dog.

My own experience is that a level-headed, sensible dog, likely to make a good worker, companion or guard, very soon gets fed up with the constant repetition of those negative exercises. Some dogs are so full of initiative and energy that they will do anything just for the sake of doing something, and I do know quite a number that have great success in competitions which without training, or in the hands of the inexperienced, would be quite unmanageable.

Even when they *are* trained, these dogs do not invariably turn out to be the sort of animals that everyone would want to keep as pets. One I know won an obedience competition with

$99\frac{1}{2}$ out of 100 marks, but in its owner's car it barks incessantly and friends given a lift are certain to be bitten—the owner herself has been nipped on occasions. And, while the dog continues to give excellent performances in the obedience ring, this state of affairs gradually gets worse. By breeding from such dogs one is likely to produce, not dogs which can be trained easily, but dogs which *must* be trained with difficulty, even if they do make excellent dogs when given some work to do.

I am not decrying obedience competitions, which have done so much to encourage training, or all the dogs which win in them. All I want to do is to emphasize that an Obedience Champion is not necessarily any more likely (he is often much less likely) to produce sensible, trainable puppies than a dog which has never achieved such an honour.

Responsibility of Ownership

Before going on to the subject of training itself, I should like to dwell a little on the question that every prospective dog owner should try to answer *honestly*, 'Is it wise for me to keep a dog at all?'

This depends, not on whether you live in a big house or a little one, in town or country, or whether you are rich or poor, young or old. It depends on one thing only—*you*, and whether or not *you* are willing to accept, and capable of accepting, your responsibilities as a dog owner. No-one is under any obligation to keep a dog, it is a responsibility you accept, not one that is forced upon you. If you fail there is only one person to blame and that's *you*! Man took the dog from Nature and has developed it for his *own* use. It is surely his duty, therefore, not only to see to its well-being, but to see that it does not interfere with the lives of his fellow men or of the other animals which they have domesticated.

The vast majority of Nature's animals belong to two classes —the hunter and the hunted—and man has domesticated both types. In the dog he has increased the ability to hunt but in the other he has removed the ability to escape. Sheep, bred for wool and mutton, *cannot* run fast enough to escape from a dog. From birds that could fly man has produced birds that lay astonishing numbers of eggs but their ability to fly is to all intents and purposes non-existent.

Whether or not it is cruel to hunt an animal bred by Nature to be hunted—whose chance of escape is usually greater than its chance of being killed, and which, if caught, meets an instantaneous death—is purely a matter of opinion. There can, however, be no doubt as to the cruelty involved in allowing a dog to worry a domesticated animal which *cannot* escape and which, far from meeting an instantaneous death, is mauled and slowly torn to pieces; probably not killed at all.

You may not like cats, but the old lady next door has just as much right to like a cat as you have to like a dog. If your dog kills her cat it is *you* who are to blame. The dog is merely following a natural instinct and you should have prevented it. You may not like cars or motor-bikes, but it is your duty to see that your dog does not become a victim to one, or that the driver of one does not become a victim to your dog.

It may be that you have a dog which cannot be trained or, more probably, that you cannot train, but you do not *have* to keep it, and if you do you must be responsible for its actions. People who do not accept these responsibilities make dogs unpopular with others. It surprises me that there are so few of the latter.

Quite apart from their duty to the nation, it is to the advantage of dog owners themselves to keep their dogs under control. Two very similar puppies can end up as two entirely different dogs. One may be allowed its freedom and will develop its instincts in its own natural way. Even if it does not get into trouble, all its interests will lie away from home, away from its owner. It will come home, of course, but no one knows when. To say that such a dog is of any value to anyone is like saying that a good husband is one who goes out in the morning to return perhaps tonight, perhaps tomorrow night, and perhaps not at all, expecting, when he does, to find food and comfort awaiting him.

Such a dog will be pleased to see its owner, who will imagine that its eyes reflect true love and devotion, whereas, in fact, it merely associates the owner with a jolly good meal and a comfortable bed. Few dogs like going on a collar and lead, but many show the greatest delight at seeing them because they associate them with going for a walk.

The other dog which is taken out, not let out, and which

is given something to do presents a very different picture. The instincts, instead of developing on their own, are kept under control. The submissive instinct becomes stronger, which means that the dog looks up to and respects its owner. Its affection increases; real affection, not just pleasure shown in return for a square meal.

Most people own one or other of the above types and have little idea of the vast difference between the two. If you own the one you will own a real dog, a friend that will honour and protect you with a courage and devotion seldom found in human friends. To own the other is merely to own an animal that lives in your house looking to you for food and comfort but finding all its other pleasures *away* from you.

There is yet another responsibility in owning a dog— responsibility to the dog itself.

I know a dog, allowed out for a walk every morning, which, at the age of twelve, was run over and had to have a leg amputated. He still takes himself for walks on three legs and his habits have become so fixed that he will never settle any other way. But is it really kind to subject our domestic animals to all the risks of modern traffic? Some people expect a dog to have 'traffic sense'. Why I do not know, as few people appear to have any! Dogs do acquire traffic sense from experience—by being run over, or nearly run over, or by very skilled training, as is practised in the training of Guide Dogs for the Blind. Even then, a high percentage of dogs are found to be unsuitable for the job, and the ordinary dog owner has not the facilities, if he has the skill, for such training. To turn a dog out with the idea that he will learn to look after himself is unfair to the dog and road users alike.

In country districts the danger is not so much from traffic as from guns. Of course it is illegal to shoot any dog unless it is *actually* worrying livestock and there is *no other means* of protecting that stock. One must try to chase the dog away and only if that fails is *anyone* within his legal right in shooting a dog. In spite of that, however, many dogs that are allowed to roam go out one day and never come back. Those of us brought up in the country have no illusions as to what happens to them. It is not what you do but what you are found out doing that provides grounds for legal action!

Not that farmers, shepherds and gamekeepers make a practice of going round looking for dogs to shoot. I have known a number of men who would shoot a dog (I consider it quite the most humane means of destruction) but I have yet to meet one who did not hate doing it. Only those who have worked with sheep seem to realize the tremendous and quite inestimable harm that a strange dog can do by just crossing a field where lambing ewes are grazing. He may be going to see a 'lady friend' with no thought of sheep on his mind. In the eyes of the law and his owners he is doing no harm and if he only does it once nothing is likely to happen to him. If it becomes a habit, however, the shepherd may be faced with the option of illegally shooting one dog, perhaps of no real value to anyone, or losing a great many valuable lambs. And don't forget that most shepherds are very fond of their sheep and resent their being ill-treated by a dog just as much as you or I would resent anyone ill-treating our dog.

To the gamekeeper the 'harmless' pet dog 'just chasing rabbits' in the hedgerows is just as great a menace, and many dogs which make a habit of it one day fail to come home. So often do dogs—good dogs too—pay the penalty of death for a crime that is entirely the owner's.

More often than not the irresponsibility of those owners arises, not through lack of consideration for others, but through a mistaken belief that they are being kind to their dog. Once I advertised a Corgi bitch on breeding terms. I pointed out that she was trained to a high standard, had great character, lots of initiative and that she would only go to someone who would appreciate these qualities. Amongst the replies was one in which the writer, in emphasizing the wonderful home he could offer, said, 'As you will see from the address, I am a Police Officer and our house adjoins fields and woods where she could hunt and roam at will.' Needless to say I did not let him have her, but that letter is an excellent example of just how irresponsible people who should know better can be in their genuine efforts to be kind to their animals.

There is another side of the picture. I feel sure that many owners find themselves in court, and many unfortunate dogs receive the death sentence as worriers, on mistaken identity. A dog I knew, a grand dog, allowed to do as he liked, created a lot of trouble by chasing cattle and the owner was warned that if it happened again she would be taken to court. Well, it did happen again, and the local P.C. was prepared to swear on oath, and in all good faith, that he had seen the same dog chasing the same cattle in the same field as before. The dog and the owner would almost certainly have been convicted on that evidence had it not been for the fact that the dog was boarding in my kennels over ten miles away, where he had been since the owner was warned! Obviously the P.C. had seen a similar dog. If those whose dogs are accused of chasing livestock were to line up several of the same breed and colour and ask the witnesses to pick out which dog it was, in nine cases out of ten they would fail. It is not sufficient, therefore, to make sure that your dog does not chase livestock. You must make equally sure that he is not *blamed* for doing so. *Take* him out—don't *let* him out.

Keeping a dog is not all pleasure; but if you have a real dog and bring him up properly you will be far more than repaid for the trouble involved. Unlike human friends, a dog will willingly give its whole life in devotion to a master, asking nothing in return. Which does not, of course, mean that it should receive nothing. Good dogs, like good wine, improve with age. They become more mellow, the responsibility of owning them decreases while the pleasure increases.

That brings us to the saddest of all responsibilities of dog ownership. You hope and can expect that, with ordinary luck, a dog will be with you for the remainder of its life. You cannot, however, expect it to be with you for the remainder of *your* life, as the average human will outlive seven average dogs.

So we come to perhaps the biggest and most difficult of all duties in owning a dog—of deciding when it would be kinder to have him put to sleep. In Nature the dog obeys the laws of the pack, which has a leader. When a member of the pack, or the pack leader himself, becomes old or infirm, it is either torn to pieces by the other members (Nature is quite unmerciful) or it crawls off to some safe hiding-place to die. Man, however, has taken the dog from Nature and, instead of following a canine pack leader, it now follows a human master. It is the duty of that master, not only to see to the mental and physical well-

PLATE VII

(a) 'No!'—followed if necessary by a tap on the nose

(b) A puppy will be quite happy in his playpen with a 'toy'

PLATE VIII

(a) Preparing to put on a
single-action slip collar
(*Sally Anne Thompson*)

(b) 'Drop it.' The dog has been
gently forced to release its hold.
For illustration purposes the fingers
of the left hand have been left in
position much longer than should
be done in practice

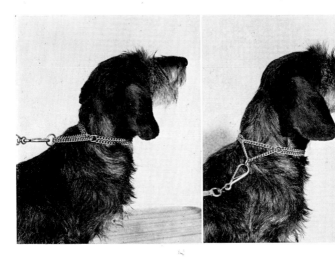

(c) Double action slip collar: *left*, long enough to prevent a choking
effect, short enough to prevent slipping over the head; *right*, short
enough to have the same tightening effect as an ordinary slip collar

being of this servant throughout its life, but also to decide when that life should come to an end.

I see many old dogs, grand old dogs, that do not live; they just exist. Thanks to the 'kindness' of their owners they are often stuffed with chocolates until they can scarcely move their bloated bodies around. Often they are covered with sores, have canker in their ears, cysts between the toes, are blind or deaf—but they cannot die. Modern science has produced drugs which keep these poor old things alive—only *just* alive.

If I, as tactfully as possible, suggest to the owners of one of those dogs that it would be much kinder to have it put to sleep, the answer is very often, 'Yes, we know that and have been talking about it for some time, but we cannot bring ourselves to do it.' That attitude, to me, is both selfish and cowardiy. These owners are not thinking of their dogs, they are thinking of *themselves*. They know perfectly well that the poor old dog should be put to sleep, but they also know that they themselves will be very upset when he goes. They will not, therefore, make the decision, in spite of the fact that they are merely postponing the evil day. If many dog lovers were to show half the courage and unselfishness towards their dog that it has shown towards them, old dogs would be saved much unnecessary and inestimable suffering.

Do not get the impression, as some people do, that we, who keep a lot of dogs, do not feel the same about losing an old favourite as you who keep only one. Good dogs, as I have said, improve with age, and those that are no good we discard before they are old. Our dogs not only live with us, they work with us too. We are just as dependant on them as they are on us. They are, in fact, an important part of our lives. As each old dog passes on, it leaves a memory that never dies, a gap that is never filled; but when any dog reaches an age when it is no longer able to enjoy life, I consider it my painful duty to have it humanely destroyed. The biggest difference between people in my position and in yours is that we have to make that awful decision far more often than you and, therefore, know only too well how difficult it is.

It is no doubt because I know this so well that I get so mad at some veterinary surgeons whose action can perhaps best be illustrated by an example. For many years we boarded a cat for some people who travelled a great deal. Because he came so frequently we treated him as one of our own and he regarded our house as another home. When he was eighteen and had been coming to us for fifteen years he came to stay for six months while his owners went abroad. He was then an old cat—but a happy, contented old cat. A few months later he returned to stay for the weekend. And he had completely changed. He wasn't ill but he was dull and had obviously lost all desire to live.

When his owner came to collect him we told her he really had reached the stage where it would be kinder to have him put to sleep. This was obviously a tremendous relief to her. She had noticed the change in the old cat and in her heart of hearts knew what was the right thing to do. Confirmation from us just gave her the courage to do it and she left us to take the old cat straight to her own vet.

A few hours later she telephoned me in a very distressed state. The vet had said there was no need to have him put down. He gave her some pills and said that if she gave him these he might live for quite a time yet. Well, he did not live—he merely existed. Fortunately he only existed for a few more weeks but they were weeks of great unhappiness to his owners.

This is no isolated example; I hear of similar cases over and over again. One's own ideas as to why vets do this sort of thing may or may not be correct. But, whatever the motive or motives, consideration for the animal is certainly not one of them. Neither is consideration for the owner. To have one's favourite dog or cat put to sleep is no easy decision to make. I think it very unkind and unfair of some veterinary surgeons to make it even more difficult.

PART II

PRACTICE

CHAPTER VII

PRINCIPLES OF TRAINING

Association of ideas—Correction and reward

Now we come to what many people will regard as the most important part of the book, but that is not my view. The easiest and best way to put anything right is to find out why it went wrong. It is easier still to prevent anything going wrong by knowing why it is likely to do so and taking appropriate precautionary measures.

It is for that reason that I have spent so much time in trying to explain what a dog is and how its mind works. All I have to say now is based on the hope that I have succeeded in explaining why a dog, without any training, will want to do certain things and, even more important, why one dog may have a tremendous desire to do something which no amount of encouragement would persuade another one to attempt.

The art of training dogs is, of course, nothing new. It is as old as the domestic dog itself. But there is little doubt that the training methods used in the old days were usually crude, often cruel and sometimes quite revolting. At that time, the dog was probably the cause of far less trouble to its owners, and other members of the community, than is its modern counterpart. Its lot, however, was not always a particularly happy one.

On the other hand, much of today's dog trouble arises from the fact that the old-fashioned 'big stick' methods of discipline have been replaced by sentimentality in everything connected with animals. In return for all that it so willingly gives, it is the duty of man to see that the lot of the domestic dog is a happier one than was that of his wild ancestors. That, however, is no reason why domestic animals and the general public, not to mention dog owners and the dogs themselves, should have to suffer because of misguided ideas of kindness. There is no doubt

G   97

that many problem dogs are merely those which have revolted against such treatment.

As so many inaccurate and misleading statements about cruelty in training are made in public, I feel that some reference should be made to it at this stage. This I do, not in the hope of converting those who adhere to the belief that all training is cruel, as others do to a political or religious belief. To try to convert such people is as futile as to attempt to convert Sir Winston Churchill to Communism. My reason for devoting space to the subject is to guide those with open minds.

One of the most common arguments put forward by the anti-trainers is that training is unnatural—an argument which shows the sort of minds they have. Man took the dog from Nature when he first domesticated it. All animals have an instinctive fear of fire. What, then, could be more unnatural than a dog on the hearth? But many dogs like to lie by the fire, and enjoy many other unnatural comforts just as much as we do. Properly trained dogs also enjoy pleasing the human master who has replaced the canine pack leader. To deny them that pleasure only makes domestication even more unnatural than it need be.

I cannot see that what constitutes cruelty, or, for that matter, kindness, can ever be anything but a matter of opinion. Many years ago I knew a lady who devoted the greater part of her life to the welfare of animals. She had a little dog which, as a youngster, had plenty of character, initiative and intelligence, for none of which he was allowed an outlet. All his owner did was to love him, very genuinely, and, fortunately or unfortunately, he had the sort of temperament that was willing to accept this life of luxury. By the time he was two years old he was so fat and lazy that he would not go for walks. So the loving owner bought a child's push-chair and took him out for 'walks' in that! Soon he was so fat that he *could* not walk and, when he was four or five years old, what little life he had left passed away.

Had I had that dog I should, on the first signs of his getting overfat, have cut down his food and *made* him go for walks, whether he wanted to or not. I should have tried to develop his initiative, instead of smothering it, by teaching him to do something, even if it were only chasing a ball. By following such a course there is no reason why this dog should not have lived (not just existed) to at least double the age he did.

Now I, and I feel sure many of my readers, have no doubt at all that my policy would have been the kinder; but no-one could have had better intentions than the kind-hearted lady who, without the slightest doubt, killed her own dog with love. Her belief that she was being kind was just as strong as is my belief that she was being unkind.

In forming *your* opinion you should remember that many statements about cruelty are made by people whose ideas on the subject are worth about as much as are my views on music. I am just as fond of music as those people are of dogs, but I have never succeeded in playing any instrument or in reading a line of music. To air my opinions on the subject would only prove how little I know!

It should also be remembered that what is great fun to one dog may be extremely unpleasant to another; one may enjoy doing something which his litter brother *cannot* do. It might, for instance, be very cruel to make one jump a certain height which to another might require no effort at all.

There is, in my opinion, no cruelty in teaching an animal to do anything of which it is mentally and physically capable, whether it be a horse pulling a load of hay or a dog walking on its hind legs. There may, however, be great cruelty in trying to force it to do something of which it is physically incapable. If its muscles have not been developed along with the training, it may strain itself and be afraid to attempt the same task in future.

On the other hand, the argument that it is impossible to teach any animal to do anything on command without the use of cruelty is no further from the truth than to say that it is impossible to train animals by cruel methods. As I have said, the methods used in bygone days were often cruel, but the dogs were undoubtedly obedient. Among present-day trainers, professional and amateur, in all fields of training, there are those whose methods I consider to be cruel or, at least, unkind. To the experienced eye the dogs themselves invariably betray the methods used, but such trainers form only a small, and ever decreasing, minority and it would be misleading to regard all training as cruel because of them.

Unfortunately, the same cannot be said of pet owners, many of whom (far too many in these enlightened times) are guilty of cruelty, usually unintentional, far in excess of anything practised by the small number of trainers to whom I have just referred. For a baby puppy to go through the night without relieving itself is as impossible as for it to jump a ten-foot wall. To punish it when it fails is just as cruel as to try to make it walk on its undeveloped hind legs, then punish it because it *cannot* do it. Oh, I know! Puppies can be 'taught' to be clean in the house that way—simply because they are *afraid* to be dirty.

I am not one of those who maintain that all dogs love being trained—some hate it. There are dogs which enjoy all their lessons but, like children, they are the exception. Few of us can say that we enjoyed every minute of our schooldays, but even fewer regret having been made to go to school. So with a dog; the pleasure a trained dog derives throughout its life outweighs any temporary displeasure it experiences in being made to do one or two exercises it dislikes. Although many dogs dislike certain exercises to begin with, there are very few which do not enjoy these same exercises once they know what is wanted.

Before reaching conclusions about cruelty in training, it is as well to think of the alternative. Every year in this nation of dog lovers thousands of dogs receive the death penalty for 'crimes' such as sheep worrying, chasing cars, biting postmen, biting their owners, straying, etc. These are the untrained dogs. The lucky ones are humanely destroyed, the unlucky meet horrible deaths, after having, perhaps, been hounded about as unwanted strays. Can that possibly be kinder than training? And don't forget the unfortunate sheep, poultry, cats, motorists and all the others who suffer as a result of untrained dogs.

In recent years, obedience training has grown tremendously in popularity, resulting in many more people training their dogs. It has also provided a means for the pooling of ideas amongst those who have studied the subject, all leading to a better understanding of the dog. Training classes are now held in most parts of the country and, if you aspire to take part in competitions, I strongly advise you to attend one. (The Kennel Club keeps a list of all societies running classes.) Even if you have no such aspirations, the fact that an experienced trainer may be able to give you first-hand advice may help to solve a problem. This is especially so with dogs that are difficult with other dogs or with people, as they can meet both at classes.

From a purely practical point of view, the standard obedience exercises, most of which originated in Germany, are entirely artificial. They do, however, give the dog which has no real work something to do, and they form the foundation for the training of all Service dogs, Police dogs, and difficult dogs sent to professional trainers. Carried out properly, they make a dog more responsive and alert—in a word, more obedient. It must be remembered, however, that one can only work on what is there, and a dog lacking the instinct, or the intelligence, to work cannot be turned into a good worker by obedience training. Nor will it *remove* undesirable traits, though it may help to keep them under control. Carried to extremes, it can kill initiative and remove individuality, so that you have an animal that does what it is told when it is told, but never does anything *until* it is told.

The majority of failures in training are due entirely to ignorance of the basic principles. These apply to the training of all animals, and, although the methods of applying them may vary, the principles themselves have never changed. As in everything else, however, methods improve and by applying up-to-date methods the same or even better results can often be achieved in weeks instead of months. Of even greater importance is the fact that the modern methods are much more humane than the old-fashioned 'big stick' methods, and I say that as one brought up to the latter and converted to the former.

The first necessity is to get right out of your head any ideas about dogs being 'almost human'. There is a word for such ideas—anthropomorphic. But you need not worry about that; just forget it and remember that *a dog is a dog* and that, fortunately, his mind works very differently from yours.

The chief difference between the canine and human mind

is that the dog does not reason as we do. Many trainers maintain that no dog ever reasons, in the sense that it never works things out in its mind; that it does not think about what it has done or what it is going to do. With that I disagree. I could give many examples of good working dogs, left to do a job without continual commands from the handler, which, I am certain, worked out in their minds the best way to tackle an unusual or difficult problem. I am quite sure that those dogs did, to a certain extent, reason, but I cannot prove it. But neither can anyone prove that they did not!

Although I believe that dogs sometimes reason, I am convinced that only dogs of exceptional intelligence do so, and then only when that intelligence is allowed or encouraged to develop. Dogs trained to a high standard of obedience, but not taught to do anything except obey commands, will merely wait for those commands and will eventually never think of using their own brain no matter how much inherent intelligence they possessed. On another point I am even more certain, and that is that practically all the wonderful examples one hears about dogs reasoning and being 'almost human' are based on what occurs, not in the mind of the dog, but in the mind of its owner!

No matter what you think, all training must be based on the assumption that DOGS DO NOT REASON, which we might call principle No. 1.

Principle No. 2 is that dogs *do not* understand every word that is said to them. They do not, in fact, understand any words at all; they merely understand sounds.

If dogs cannot reason and do not understand words, why do they do what they are told and how can they be taught to do so? They learn by ASSOCIATION OF IDEAS; the dog associates certain reactions with pleasure or displeasure and, not surprisingly, tends to follow the reaction which provides the former and refrain from doing anything which provokes the latter.

The first association created by a certain experience is always stronger and more lasting than subsequent associations. An example of this is well known to exhibitors of show dogs. Puppies cannot be shown until six months old but, even then, the first show is often a bewildering or terrifying experience. If, at its first show, a puppy has no unpleasant experiences, its next show may not be so bad and soon it should take everything in its stride. Lots of unpleasant things, however, can happen at its first show, the most likely being that it will have to be handled (mauled is often a more apt word) by a judge who knows all about show points but who just hasn't a clue as to how to approach and handle a dog. Other risks are being trodden on by exhibitors, or attacked by some dog not under proper control. If any, or all, of these things happen to a puppy at its *first* show, it may be put off shows *for life* and I am confident that the chances of many excellent dogs are completely ruined by a very unpleasant experience of one sort or another at their first show. A puppy that has been to several shows, and begun to enjoy showing, may have an unpleasant experience which can put it off for a time. It will not, however, have anything like the lasting effect it would have had it happened at the puppy's *first* show.

As the dog cannot tell us, we cannot be sure how the associations form in its mind, but it is pretty certain that they do so in very much the same way as they do in our own. Most of us associate certain experiences, often for years afterwards, with something we saw, heard or felt at the time. It may be a catchy tune or a moonlit night; it may be an air-raid warning or a boy with a telegram which we associate with past events, pleasant or unpleasant. The more pleasant or unpleasant they were the stronger and more lasting will the association be, the strongest usually being those associated with fear.

Even when experiences are neither very pleasant nor unpleasant we may associate them with something which occurs over and over again. The retired soldier, for instance, will immediately associate a certain bugle call with something he always did in response to it.

Perhaps of greater importance is the fact that it is impossible to tell what sort of associations will be built up; two people may associate the same experience with something entirely different. Two people might be involved in the same motor accident. One may be reminded of it every time she hears the screech of brakes, while it may come back to the other every time she sees a car of the make involved in the accident.

The same applies to dogs, except that dogs, being unable to reason, cannot be made to realize that something which happened today is unlikely to happen again. A dog simply associates a certain experience with something it sees, hears or feels—nothing more and nothing less. That is a great help in training, but unwanted and unexpected associations do develop at times, giving rise to much misunderstanding and confusion. I shall, therefore, try to give a most unlikely example of what *could* happen. You have a puppy between six and twelve months old (usually a very impressive age) which goes happily on a lead and you take it down the street. On walking under a ladder (you are not superstitious!) a workman drops something on the pup, hurting it only slightly but giving it a terrible fright. What happens then? The most likely thing is that he will associate this dreadful experience with a ladder; being terrified to go under one again. But he might have noticed a man on the ladder and only be afraid of a ladder with a man on it. Or he might associate the experience with the shop in front of which the ladder stood, and be afraid to go past it, even when there is no ladder there. Or he might associate the shop *and* the ladder, being quite happy to pass the former if the latter is not there and not afraid to go under a ladder in front of any other shop.

These are the most likely associations, and are unlikely to create a big problem. What could present a very great problem is that the puppy might associate this experience with *you*, especially if he is a new pup. As you cannot explain that you had no part in the affair, it may take a long time and a great deal of patience to regain his confidence, particularly when you take him for a walk. If you are very unlucky, he might have another fright next time you take him out, completely shattering his confidence in you. Through no fault of your own he may become terrified of you, simply because he associates you with a terrifying experience.

For the purpose of training we provide pleasure or displeasure, according to whether we want the dog to do something or not to do something. The associations of ideas are built up by what is known as correction and reward. All training is based on correction and reward, and, in my opinion, the 'gift' of being able to train animals is due, almost entirely, to the ability to apply the correction or reward *at the right time,* to apply the type of correction or reward most effective on the animal in question and to strike a balance between the two suitable to the individual animal.

Because of their importance I shall now try to explain what is meant by correction and reward. Correction, as applied in training, is very often a misnomer. The anti-training crank, scanning the pages of this book for evidence of cruelty, will no doubt conjure up a picture of me, the great brute, beating the life out of some tiny puppy. To the successful trainer, correction probably means nothing more than pushing a dog into some desired position. It might, in the first place, be described as any action on the part of the trainer either to make a dog do something by force or to restrain it from doing something, again by force.

By applying correction in conjunction with a signal the dog can hear (a word of command) or see (a hand signal), the dog will in time learn to associate this signal with the correction and, in anticipation, should carry out the movement on hearing and/ or seeing it *before* the correction has been applied. For example, you say 'Sit', followed by the action of pushing the dog into a sitting position. If it is an easy dog you will find, after repeating this several times, that on hearing 'Sit' the dog will place itself in the sitting position before you have pushed it. The same applies if you give a hand signal. In an effort to make everything as easy as possible for the dog, in the initial stages I use both hand signal and word of command. Another example: if you say 'No' as the dog does, or is about to do, something wrong, followed by correction (this time in a more severe form), it will learn, on hearing the word 'No', to refrain from carrying out that particular act.

It is, of course, just as easy to teach a dog to sit by saying 'Stand' or 'Get up', or to refrain from doing something by saying 'Yes'. Dogs do not understand any words, and if you always use the same sound for a particular action the dog will soon associate that sound with the action and, by reacting to it, will obey a word of command.

There are many different methods of applying correction. The method used should depend on the dog and on what you are trying to teach. What would be a mild form of correction to one dog might be severe punishment to another; while the efforts of some owners to apply correction is regarded by their boisterous young dogs as a huge joke!

In modern obedience training most correction is applied by the lead through the slip collar; this is the only method I use in teaching the elementary exercises, 'heel work', 'sits and downs' and 'recall'. The advantages of this method (explained more fully later) are that it can be applied instantly and, just as important, the dog is as quickly released from the correction. It can also be applied in any degree to suit a particular dog, so that you can give the merest suggestion of a jerk to a sensitive dog or jerk an insensitive one right off its feet.

Remember that correction and punishment are very different things. To get a dog to do what you want it to do correction is necessary, but a dog should *never* be punished unless it is *deliberately* disobedient. As it cannot be deliberately disobedient until it knows right from wrong, no dog should ever be punished until you have taught it what is right and what is wrong. Neither should any dog ever be punished because you *think* he is being deliberately disobedient. Just because he did the right thing yesterday it does not follow that he understood the command—it may have happened by chance—and to punish him because he does wrong today is not only cruel but will cause the dog to distrust you. No success in training will ever be achieved if a dog does not trust its owner. If you think he *should* know but are not quite sure that he *does*, always give the dog the benefit of the doubt.

Punishment, although applied for a different reason, may take the form merely of severe correction by the slip collar. I usually use another method, not commonly used in obedience training circles but often used by sheepdog and gundog trainers. It is to pick the dog up, either by the scruff or the loose skin under the throat, and shake him. In the case of a hard dog you can pick him up, glare at him straight in the face, and *really* shake him. Don't forget that, though no physical pain is inflicted, this is a very severe form of punishment. Don't forget, either, that dogs hate being stared at and to a trained one a 'look' can be just as effective as a word of command.

Man is able to control animals, often much more powerful than himself, because of his ability to reason and their inability to do so. This enables him to give the impression that he is more powerful than they, and what could be more likely to give that impression to a dog than to pick it up and shake it? Some dogs are, of course, too big to pick right off their feet and, in the case of a hard one, a good thump in the ribs with the clenched fist while you pull him up to you, glaring at him, often serves to drive the lesson home. That does, of course, inflict a certain amount of physical pain, but if you watch show-jumping you will see riders 'using their legs', as it is termed in horses, in which they actually kick the horses harder on both sides than the average dog owner could possibly thump a dog. If they did not, many would not get over the first obstacle and, unless you can make your dog understand that he *must* do what you say, you will fail to negotiate the obstacles almost certain to be met in the course of training.

The two most important points to note in the application of correction or punishment are:

(1) The object is not to apply them to the body as so many people imagine, but to the mind. The only way to get at some dogs' minds is to make it painful, or at least unpleasant, for them to refuse to pay attention; but a great deal of the physical punishment that is inflicted on dogs is unnecessary and does harm, not good. Because it is the mind we are trying to get at, I use, on occasion, what I call shock tactics, which make the dog momentarily afraid to be disobedient. These (explained more fully later) must be applied with great care and *never* to a timid dog or young puppy.

(2) *Never* use a 'weapon' of any sort and never raise your hand to smack a dog. The only time I ever hit a dog is in applying some of the shock tactics. Then it is a sudden, swift flick, designed to surprise, or even frighten (the dog should not know where it came from), but not to hurt.

Practically all owners of 'problem dogs' have smacked them either with their hand or a weapon such as a folded newspaper, a whip, a stick or a lead. These methods usually have one of two effects:

(1) The dog associates the punishment with the owner not the 'crime' and therefore loses confidence in its owner. Often do I hear remarks such as 'When I got him at eight weeks he was as bold as brass but now he seems so nervous.' Would we not all

be nervous if, as infants, someone had 'shooed' us all over the place walloping us with a folded newspaper?

(2) In the bold 'pack leader' type of dog, such methods breed defiance and are accepted as a challenge. Instead of morally overpowering the dog, by picking it up, we challenge it physically at its own level—and it nearly always wins! A smack with the hand will often have the same effect as a kick from a bullock or a bite from a rat—it incites the dog to retaliate. What is more, a clever dog does not often get kicked or bitten a second time, and the clever dog will soon learn to evade wild swipes by an irate owner!

Generally speaking, only the minimum of correction should be applied and 'if at first you don't succeed' gradually apply more and more until you do. That rule should not, however, always be applied to punishment, if there is a risk of bad habits developing. It is sometimes better and kinder to punish a dog *once* really severely than to go on punishing him mildly for a long time.

For instance, a young dog may suddenly decide to chase a boy on a bicycle, rushing from you towards the bicycle, then coming back towards you barking furiously at the cyclist. Here is an opportunity that may never arise again and should on no account be lost, as you may be able to catch the dog as it passes you with its whole mind and body in the act of chasing a bicycle. If this is the *first* time this dog has ever chased a bicycle you may, by seizing this golden opportunity, and the dog, and nearly shaking the 'living daylight' out of him, cure him of chasing bicycles *for life*. If, however, you merely reprimanded such a dog, the pleasure he derived from chasing the bicycle might be greater than the displeasure caused by the reprimand. This means that he will chase the next bicycle he sees when, of course, you can apply more severe punishment. But, as the instinct to chase develops, so the pleasure derived from chasing increases. It may continue to increase at a pace exceeding the increasing displeasure from the more and more severe punishment you administer, perhaps ending up with a dog that has to be kept on a lead to prevent its getting into serious trouble.

Reward can take several forms. Anything which provides pleasure is reward, but, in dogs, as in humans, a pleasant experience to one may be an equally unpleasant experience to another. Food is the most common reward used by the average pet owner, but the only type of professional training in which it is generally used is with performing dogs for stage or circus acts. Trainers of sheepdogs, gundogs and police dogs rarely use food, and then only sparingly. Some condemn its use in any circumstances. These trainers are apt to overlook the fact that they have at their disposal a source of pleasure which the companion dog owner is usually denied. To any animal (sometimes including ourselves) the greatest pleasures are derived from one or other of the instincts, and to a dog bred to herd sheep, to retrieve, to kill vermin, etc., there is no pleasure so great as being allowed to work. But it is unlikely that you will be able to work your dog and very likely that, at some time, you will have to curb his tendencies to do so. For that reason you will have to resort to some other method of reward if you want him not only to do what he is told, when he is told, but to enjoy doing it.

Food is often an added incentive to do something a little bit more quickly and more gleefully. In the early training of little puppies I have found it helpful, but it should be noted that a dog which does something merely because a piece of meat is dangled before its nose is not, in fact, an obedient dog. It should also be noted that some dogs are quite indifferent to tit-bits, while others are so greedy that the thought of the piece of biscuit in your pocket will occupy their minds so completely that it is impossible to get them to think about the lesson in hand.

The other instinct through which you can reward your dog is the submissive instinct, which makes the dog so much more easily trained than the equally intelligent domestic pet, the cat. As I have emphasized, the average dog *wants* a leader and, although rare, there are dogs which can be taught to do anything within their power solely to please their trainer. The owner can provide pleasure through the submissive instinct, and encourage it to develop, simply by showing that he is himself pleased. In training it is not enough to show that you are pleased when the dog does what you want; you must leave him in no doubt whatsoever that you are absolutely delighted *if he makes the slightest attempt to do what you want.* But don't keep on fussing him when he has done nothing to deserve it.

As with correction, it is necessary to teach a dog to associate a certain sound with reward. If, as you fuss over him, you tell him he is a 'good boy', 'good dog' or whatever you like, he will learn to associate these words of praise with reward and with doing right, and you will then be able to praise him at a distance.

Of greater importance than how to apply correction and reward is the striking of a balance between the two. In contrast to the people who contend that dogs can be trained only by love and affection, I meet people who believe, just as strongly, that too much affection spoils a dog. I know owners of excellent working dogs who never say a kind word to them or give them a friendly pat, maintaining that to do so would spoil them. For long I have been convinced that those who hold this belief not only fail to get the best out of their dog, good though it may be, but that they also lose the pleasure of owning a dog that works *with* a master rather than *for* one. Dogs are spoiled not by too much affection, but by too little correction and by continual petting for no reason at all. To this they become so accustomed that they expect, almost demand, it as their right.

It is all a question of balance. No matter how severely you have to punish your dog he will not dislike you if he *knows* for what he is being punished and if you are equally lavish with your reward when he does right, or even tries to do right.

When to apply correction and reward is far more important than *how*. If the dog is going to associate pleasure or displeasure with something he should or should not do, the pleasure, in the form of reward, or displeasure, in the form of correction, must be applied *when his mind is on a particular act*. As an example, take a dog chasing a rabbit which goes to ground. The dog looks down the burrow, decides it isn't worth the bother and goes back to its owner. That is common among dogs that are neither corrected nor rewarded but just left to do as they like.

Supposing, however, the owner wanted to stop such a dog chasing rabbits. First of all, before the dog made any actual move in the direction of the rabbit, its mind told it to do so. Secondly, the owner, if he or she were alert and really knew the dog, could and should anticipate this action and be able to correct the dog just as it formed the intention of setting off in pursuit of the rabbit. Correction applied at the right psychological moment, just as the dog decides to do the wrong thing, is the most effective of all. If the dog can be corrected as it proceeds, hell for leather, after the rabbit, that will also be effective; as will be correction applied if the dog can be caught with his head *and his mind* half-way down the rabbit burrow.

The dog, however, eventually decides that he has had enough, but *before* his body moves out of the burrow its mind must instruct it to do so. It is possible, and indeed probable, that the dog has already decided to go back to its master and, to correct it after that decision has been made, is correcting the dog, not for chasing rabbits, but for going back to its owner. We then have a dog which chases rabbits, for which it has never been corrected, but refuses to go back to its owner because it has been corrected for that.

Correction and reward must, therefore, be applied either as the dog does right or wrong, or as he is thinking of doing so. It must always be borne in mind that in its own mind the untrained dog never does either right or wrong; it merely obeys instincts. Therefore, the first task of the trainer is to make it clear to the dog what he considers to be wrong, and that can be done only by correcting the animal when its mind is on the subject. Exactly the same applies to reward.

As the trainer controls correction and reward, there is less likelihood of wrong associations developing, as in the case of the puppy and the ladder. The risk, however, is ever present, and the most experienced trainers sometimes find that the dog has got things the wrong way round. For no reason that we know, an association may start to form in the least expected direction. The thing to do, on the first indication of that happening, is *stop*. Change to another method, use another word of command, discontinue training altogether until you can get some advice, do anything you can think of—but don't keep struggling on in the wrong direction.

We have now divided the principles of training into (1) Dogs do not reason; (2) Dogs do not understand any words; (3) Dogs learn by the association of ideas; (4) Man builds up that association by correction and reward; (5) The reward or correction must be applied when the dog's mind is on doing right or wrong.

The following examples may help to show you how they work:

Example No. 1

You say to your dog 'Going for a walk' and he gets wildly excited. Not because he understands the phrase as you or I understand it, but simply because he associates the sound with the pleasure of going for a walk. More than likely he simply associates the sound 'walk' with pleasure and may get just as excited if you say casually to your wife or husband, 'How about going out for a walk?' An intelligent, wide-awake dog will pick up and associate many such sounds, but that is no reason why you should think, as so many dog owners do, that he understands your conversation.

He may get just as excited at the sight of your picking up his lead or putting on your coat and hat. The greatest pleasure shown by our own team of demonstration dogs was when they went out to give displays. As soon as they realized we were going somewhere, pandemonium prevailed. Quite apart from the noise, many of them refused to eat and we therefore made every effort to hide from them the fact that anything unusual was taking place—with little success. Soon a beam of delight would show in the eyes of one of the brighter dogs, followed by others, until one of the noisy ones started shouting, as it were, 'We're going out today, boys and girls!' and from then on there was a complete uproar. Some dogs have an almost uncanny ability to spot anything unusual and it is very rarely that we know what they have noticed. But the majority just follow the leader. This is partly due to the pack instinct and partly due to the fact that, although not so quick in spotting something unusual for themselves, they associate the excitement of the others with the pleasure of going out and, therefore, get excited too.

Another fact which dog owners do not always appreciate is that dogs know the time of day and will associate a certain time with a pleasant or unpleasant experience, provided it happens regularly. The human being is the only one of the higher animals which requires a watch to tell the time, and the more primitive humans still do not require it. Cows that are milked at a regular time each day will congregate around the gate almost to the minute, and hens which are fed regularly will hang around waiting for their food. If, therefore, your dog knows what time the postman calls, the children come home from school, or when he has his last run at night, he is merely showing that he is as clever as the average cow or hen!

Example No. 2

Mr. Knowsitall takes his four-months-old puppy 'Trouble' for a walk in the park. Trouble is a nice bouncing pup full of the joys of life and has a wonderful romp by himself until, in the distance, he sees Miss Lovadog with Popsy. Trouble decides to make her acquaintance and dashes off in that direction. Eventually Mr. Knowsitall awakens to the fact that Trouble is not just racing round in a circle but is heading straight for Miss Lovadog and Popsy. He starts shouting: 'Trouble, come here! *Trouble*, do you hear me! TROUBLE, you * * ! ! *.' If Trouble does hear he certainly gives no indication; and why should he? He has not been taught to associate these sounds with anything. To him they are just noises, like those he has been growing accustomed to on the radio, and he proceeds on his way as fast as his podgy legs will carry him.

Suddenly Miss Lovadog sees this 'savage' animal approaching and, with a blood-curdling scream, grabs hold of dear Popsy. But Trouble is accustomed to the radio and is not deterred by a scream which, to him, is just another noise that means nothing. Being a *real* pup he throws his boisterous self wholeheartedly into the spirit of the game, jumping up at poor Popsy, rushing round barking and having a good old tug at Miss Lovadog's skirt in passing.

Puppies, like children, do not play the same game for long and, in a few minutes, Trouble decides he has had enough of that for the time being. He decides to go back to his master, who has by now proceeded about half-way towards him. So he looks round, spots his master and off he goes, a bit exhausted but as happy as only a playful puppy can be, straight up to Mr. Knowsitall. What does Mr. Knowsitall do? He gives the poor little devil a good hiding in the belief that he is punishing him for being disobedient and running away.

What has he done? First of all Mr. Knowsitall, having

H

made no attempt to teach his puppy right from wrong, is punishing it for doing something which it can not know was wrong. Secondly he has punished it, not for running away, but for coming back, and no one can blame it if it is very chary about going back to him in future. Thirdly, and most important of all, this puppy has gone back, in all good faith, to its master, whom, more than anyone else, it should be able to trust. But what reward does it get? A hiding, probably far more severe than would be necessary in the case of an adult dog that *had* been deliberately disobedient. The result of such a cruel and stupid action is that any confidence the puppy had in its master is immediately lost. It will associate going to its master, not with pleasure, but with displeasure and it will as far as possible avoid doing so.

That, however, is not all the harm that can be done. Mr. Knowsitall is actually *teaching* his puppy to be disobedient. By constantly repeating its name he is teaching it to associate this sound either with nothing in particular or with something in the distance which may be worth investigating. I have seen dogs, particularly fighters, which, the moment they are called, look round to see where the other dog is; simply because they associate this sound, not with going to their owners, but with a rival to fight.

Example No. 3

Mr. and Mrs. A. have a young dog called Bonzo and they go out, leaving him alone in the house. On their return, they receive the usual warm welcome from Bonzo, who is then let out into the garden while Mrs. A. gets the supper. After supper she goes upstairs and discovers that, during their absence, Bonzo has amused himself by tearing the rug on the landing to pieces. She is very angry and calls Mr. A. who says, 'I'll teach him not to do that,' but Mrs. A. says: 'Oh but if you spank him now he may not know what it is for. That book we bought says that the dog should not be punished unless it knows what it is for.' To this Mr. A. replies: 'I bet he knows all right. As a matter of fact, I thought he looked a bit guilty when we came in. Just you wait and see what he does now,' and proceeds to the garden where Bonzo lies peacefully asleep. Mr. A. then fixes the poor dog with an icy stare and in a very gruff voice

says, 'Who tore up the rug?', whereupon Bonzo looks rather
cowed. 'There,' says Mr. A., 'see how guilty he looks. He
knows perfectly well what I mean,' and proceeds to wallop
him.

It is possible, but highly improbable, that Bonzo did know
for what he was being punished. Why then should he look
guilty? He did not; he merely looked afraid. If you own a dog
and want to prove this, all you have to do is to look at him with
a ferocious stare and say to him in a very angry voice, 'Who
tore up the rug?', 'Abracadabra' or anything else you fancy,
and see what happens. It is almost certain that your dog will
look just as guilty as Bonzo. He looks afraid for either or both
of two reasons: (1) He has been taught to associate this harsh
tone of voice with doing the wrong thing and, therefore,
associates it with correction or punishment, or (2) a dog
instinctively reacts to a harsh tone of voice by cowering as it
would if a canine pack leader growled at it.

The results of such treatment are, firstly, that the dog is
not one little bit reformed so far as tearing up rugs is concerned, as he does not associate the punishment with the crime.
In the second place, he is quite likely to associate the home-
coming of his owners with punishment. Instead of his usual
warm welcome, he will greet them, if not with fear, certainly
with a good deal of apprehension.

From the above I hope you will have formed some idea,
not only of how associations of ideas are formed, but of how
easy it is to form wrong associations, against which you must
be continually on your guard.

There are a number of definite rules which apply to all
training.

Correction and reward should be applied according to
whether the dog does right or wrong, not whether you feel in
a good or a bad mood.

If you do have an 'argument', have it out there and then
and finish up on friendly terms. If you do have to punish a dog,
make a point of immediately getting him to do something for
which you can praise him.

Don't 'keep on' at him for hours or days, saying: 'Who was
a naughty boy?' 'Who left a pool on the carpet?', or, worse still,
'sending him to Coventry'.

Never threaten a dog or tell him what you will do if he doesn't behave. Do IT, and be done with it.

Never miss an opportunity to correct a dog for doing what you don't want him to do, to reward him for doing what you do want done, and to nip any possible bad habits in the bud.

Remember that, besides the bad habits which are so easily acquired, there are good habits which should be encouraged from the start.

Don't keep on trying a 'cure' which has no effect. Often, owners of dogs which do something they shouldn't say to me, 'I smack him *every* time he does it but it has not the slightest effect.' Then why smack him? If you are sure that certain tactics are having no effect, change them quickly or you may be teaching your dog to be disobedient.

Make the fullest possible use of the dog's intelligence but do not over-estimate it. Many dogs are punished for disobedience by owners who have failed to make them understand what they should and should not do.

Never ask your dog to do something when you know perfectly well he won't. If you give an order which is obeyed you have gone a step forward; if you give an order which is disobeyed you have gone a step back, but if you don't give an order at all you will merely stand still. We don't want to stand still, but it is always better than going backwards. One of the first essentials in training is to avoid giving the dog the opportunity to disobey.

Don't get into the habit of shouting at your dog. That only makes people think you are a bully, and you will be throwing away what may, on occasions, prove a very valuable aid to control. If you teach your dog to obey quiet commands you will, in an emergency, be able to raise the tone of voice. This will attract the dog's attention, but if you make a habit of shouting he will become accustomed to the noise and you will have nothing to fall back on in an emergency.

Above all, be just and fair at all times, remembering that, although there is no harm in a dog being afraid of doing wrong, he should *never* be afraid of his owner. I have seen owners coax a dog up to them in reassuring tones, then grab and punish it. Dogs think as little as I do of people who play such dirty tricks.

If you can turn the whole of your dog's training into one

big game, so much the better. The point to bear in mind is that *you* must control the game and say when it is time to stop. A dog can quite easily develop a mania for certain things, such as retrieving sticks and stones. To such an extent can this develop that many dogs do not go for a walk with their owners, the owner goes for a walk with the dog, to spend his or her time throwing sticks and stones. Refusal to do so results in jumping up at the owner, and incessant barking, apart from which it is very difficult to teach such a dog anything else. Once this, or any other habit, has become an obsession it is almost impossible to get the dog to listen to what you are saying to him, far less to concentrate on his lessons.

CHAPTER VIII

THE NEW PUPPY

Settling down and making friends—House-training—Learning its name
and coming when called—Chewing—Collar and lead—Being left alone
—Jumping up—Pestering

Now let us tackle this dog of yours on the principles outlined
in the previous chapter. As most owners start with a young
puppy I shall begin with one of, say, eight weeks, reared in
kennels with brothers and sisters. I am assuming that you have
followed the advice already given and bought a trainable
puppy. Not a perfect one, but one with intelligence and a good
temperament. I have no intention of telling you how to deal
with 'problem' dogs but only how to prevent a trainable dog
becoming a problem.

Before taking it home it is a good idea to prepare some sort
of enclosure, big enough to allow a reasonable amount of
freedom and strong enough to keep in the puppy you have in
mind. This pen need not be large or elaborate; the puppy will
not spend its life there. Any handyman can make a portable
pen, on the lines of a child's playpen, which can be moved
indoors or out. In the pen should be a bed—a box on its side
is ideal. (*See* Plate VII [*b*].) The advantages of this pen I shall
be explaining as we proceed.

The first, and probably the most important, fact to remember is that, although far more intelligent and capable of
fending for itself than we were at eight weeks, your puppy is
still a baby.

All young creatures, on two legs or four, have certain things
in common. Firstly they want plenty of nourishing food and
plenty of sleep. They should be kept warm when asleep,
although if healthy they will never catch cold when running
about. They also want freedom to run and develop their
muscles but should never be forced to run until exhausted.
They need freedom to develop their brain, too, and at this

stage it will develop much better if you *allow* rather than try to *make* it do so.

Above all, they want a protector to whom they can run in time of danger, real or imaginary. Man has taken the dog from Nature and you have taken this puppy from its mother, brothers and sisters. You have, therefore, taken upon yourself (no-one has forced it upon you) the role of mother, guardian, pack leader or however you care to regard it. The puppy will look to you for affection, protection and guidance. And don't forget that in the natural state dogs *do not* do what they like, they obey their pack leader and your puppy will actually *want* you to tell him what to do.

What I want to emphasize most of all at this stage is the importance of building up confidence and mutual trust between you and the puppy. No success will ever be achieved in training, and no pleasure derived by either dog or owner, unless they trust each other. Once a dog's confidence is shaken, as frequently happens quite by accident, it can be regained only by showing the dog that you really meant no harm, which takes time and patience. Far better, therefore, not to do anything likely to lose the puppy's confidence.

A common problem arises on the first night a puppy goes to a new home—and howls! Should you scold it, leave it alone, or feel sorry for it and take it to bed with you? If you scold it you may shake its confidence and, anyhow, who would scold a baby for being unhappy? If you take it to bed it will be happy and tomorrow night will howl in anticipation of the same reward. The best thing is to leave it alone, when it should very soon give up howling as a bad job. You should, of course, make it as comfortable as possible. Many puppies seem to miss the warmth of their brothers and sisters as much as the company. A hot-water bottle wrapped up in a blanket often has a miraculous effect in getting a puppy to settle down and go to sleep. Often it helps if one stays with the puppy, stroking it gently until it goes to sleep, then moving quietly away.

Remember that this puppy is going to associate you and your home with either pleasure or displeasure. Although the infant mind is less retentive than the adult's, the first impression a puppy gets of its new home is going to stick in its mind much more than those which come later. For that reason it is most important not to apply any form of correction, or do anything which may frighten the puppy, until it has settled down and accepted you as a friend. It may do that right away, but I am sure that many nervous dogs are made that way during the first week in a new home.

That is not intended as an excuse for bad temperaments, which would be the same no matter how the dogs were treated. There are, however, many not-so-bold dogs which would, with proper treatment, develop confidence as they grew older. Instead, what little confidence they have is knocked out of them by people who think they must start 'training' their baby puppy the moment they get it home. In common with most other professional trainers, when I get a dog to train I do no training for at least a week (much longer is sometimes necessary), during which time he settles down and gets to know me.

Quite often I am asked, 'What age should I start training?' and 'Is he too old to train?'

Dogs, like us, learn all their lives, although, again like us, some are rather unwilling to do so! Some breeders talk to their puppies and handle them whenever they start feeding, thus teaching them to associate a human voice and touch with something pleasant. Puppies so treated will settle down and accept a new owner much more quickly than those which simply have their food pushed at them and their kennels cleaned out by a commercially minded owner. Strictly speaking, training starts in these cases at about three weeks.

On the other hand, dogs *can* be trained at any age. Quiz, an Alsatian, who became well known for her Police Dog Displays, was going to be destroyed, and was given to me as unmanageable at three and a half years. She was, however, much more difficult to train than if I had had her as a puppy; not because of her age but because of the bad habits she had got into. The old saying that you can't teach an old dog new tricks is not true. I have taught dogs of eight years and over to do something they had never done before (to do something in a film for instance) in a few days. These were, however, 'educated' dogs; to teach a completely untrained dog of that age would take much longer. To teach one which, besides being untrained, had developed bad habits would take much longer still.

Young puppies have not very retentive minds—what you

teach today may well be forgotten tomorrow. For that reason few professional trainers like to take a dog until it is getting on for a year old when it can be trained more quickly and is more likely to remember what it has been taught. But many dogs would never have to go to professionals if their owners would prevent their developing bad habits as puppies.

For these reasons my advice is: (1) prevent bad habits developing and encourage good ones when they begin to appear, which may be at six weeks or never at all; (2) apart from that, the less training you give a puppy until he 'grows up' (mentally) the better will his character and individuality develop; (3) a dog is never too old to learn, but I think it is unkind to let a dog become set in his ways, then, when he is old, suddenly try to change those ways.

Here we come to the first advantage of the playpen. There are few households where anyone has the time to keep a constant eye on a puppy, and little ones are adept at getting under one's feet, often being trodden on accidentally. Some puppies don't seem to mind and soon learn to keep out of the way, but others will associate the unpleasant experiences, especially if they occur soon after arrival in a new home, with the new owner, the new home or with human beings in general. These risks can easily be avoided by putting the puppy in its pen when you are busy, where he can relax and go to sleep (most important in a baby puppy) instead of being constantly chivvied around.

If a puppy gets into mischief and you don't correct it, you may be allowing a bad habit to develop. If you correct it before it has gained confidence in you, it may never gain that confidence. If, however, you put it in a pen, it *cannot* get into mischief. You will thereby avoid two risks—the puppy getting into bad habits or losing confidence in you.

Another point is that by giving a puppy a bed in its pen it will come to regard that bed as its own property. When, later on, you take away the pen or move the bed, it is quite likely that the puppy will go to bed without any training. Even if it does not, it is much easier to teach a pup to go to its *own* bed —and stay there—than to teach it to lie in a bed it has never seen before.

Let us now imagine that you have just arrived home with

your puppy. It is more than likely that it will show signs of bewilderment in its new surroundings and perhaps be inclined to scuttle into a corner, or under a chair, at the sound of unusual noises. At this stage the important point to remember is to *let* it, rather than try to *make* it, get accustomed to its new surroundings and to members of the household. Whatever you do, *don't chase it*. Right from the start get the puppy to come to you and see that it always associates coming to you with pleasure. Any healthy puppy enjoys tit-bits but even more does a puppy, especially a strange and bewildered one, want affection. In spite of all that some working-dog men say about spoiling dogs and making them 'soft', baby puppies love to be cuddled and I have yet to find that it does them any harm. At the same time, many puppies are encouraged to be afraid by owners who sympathize too much in all their 'little ordeals'; who unintentionally praise the puppy for being afraid. Without being unsympathetic, always try to give the impression that there is really nothing to fear.

Any untrained animal has certain instinctive reactions to other animals, including ourselves. Our intentions for good or evil are transmitted to an animal chiefly by three different means—the tone of voice, the touch of the hand and the movement of the body or hand, especially in approaching the animal.

An animal that is afraid may often be calmed by talking to it quietly in a firm, calm tone of voice. Shouting in a harsh tone will cause it to become even more afraid, and the same will happen if the person concerned is also afraid and displays that fear in the tone of voice. It is not what you say but how you say it that matters. Tone of voice is of the greatest importance throughout training.

The touch of the hand is equally important. I have seen dogs which, through fear, would snap at the approach of my hand, relax when I got hold of them and stroked them gently. There are two common mistakes which people make in this connection. The first is that they clutch at the dog. This may hurt it and will almost certainly give it a feeling of being caught, which any frightened animal will instinctively fight against. Obviously, if it is afraid you will have to hold it firmly or it will escape. But, although difficult to explain on paper, there is all the difference in the world between a firm, gentle hold and gripping or clutching. The second mistake is patting instead of stroking. Most dogs enjoy a friendly pat from their master, but the puppy we are discussing has no master, and no confidence will be transmitted through the patting of a stranger. Stroke gently but firmly, especially on the head, the cheeks or behind the ears, and the puppy should gradually relax. Dogs hate being patted on the head, although many are forced to tolerate it.

In approaching an animal it is quite astonishing how people manage to invent so many methods which they should *never* use. The commonest mistakes arise from the facts that all dogs hate being stared at, and that they view with suspicion anyone who falters in his or her approach. The answer is simple—don't stare and don't hesitate.

There seems to be a widespread belief that every dog wants to play boisterous games with everybody it meets. Why a dog should want to play with a complete stranger I just cannot think, but many people expect it to do so. They jump about in front of it or poke at it in fun, but few dogs appear to find this funny. A timid dog will be afraid of such an idiot, while an aggressive one will want to attack. Children will play together or with an adult once they know each other, but there are few indeed who will want to play the moment they meet a complete stranger—so why should a dog?

Although it is not quite correct to say that you should start as you intend to continue, it is, at this stage, a very good idea to decide *how* you do intend to continue. For instance, I come across people who allow a cuddly puppy to sleep on their lap or on their bed, but, when it grows into a whacking great Alsatian or Boxer, they curse it for having got into the habit of doing so.

While on the subject of habit it is worth remembering that, apart from the bad habits which are so easily acquired, there are also good habits which should be encouraged from the start.

A common problem which besets the family which owns a dog is 'Who should do the training?' The answer depends chiefly on the family itself, but I may be able to help in arriving at a decision. A dog will obey any number of people it knows, trusts and respects, if they all use the same commands in as near as possible the same tone of voice. It will not, however, be equally obedient with them all, for two reasons: (1) The natural 'command' which people have over dogs varies and, while one person can easily control a whole pack, another cannot control even one of the same dogs; (2) Dogs become attached to the person who trains them and will obey that person in preference to any other.

To make things as easy as possible for the dog, it is better for one person to do the initial training, particularly the disciplinary exercises. Once he has grasped the meaning of a command, there is no reason why he should not obey it when given by other members of the family. You must, of course, use a little common sense, and if, when one member of the family has the dog out, he chases a cat it is no good saying, 'I mustn't punish him; Dad is doing the training.' By the time Dad has an opportunity to catch the puppy in the act the hunting instinct may have developed to such an extent that he cannot suppress it.

Although a dog *may* be under the control of *any* member of the family, it *should* be under the control of *one* only. Don't, please don't, all give commands at the same time. Instead of a clear word of command, a sound easily understood, the dog hears a babble that means nothing. Just imagine a lot of people trying to tell you something at the same time. What is the first thing you do? You say very firmly, 'One at a time, *please*,' and, if dogs could speak, that would be a common plea.

House-Training

The first thing everyone wants to teach a puppy is to be clean in the house. This should be started right away. If it can be persuaded to develop the good habit of going out to relieve itself it should prove no further trouble, whereas if it develops the bad habit of using the best carpet for the same purpose it may be extremely difficult to cure.

It seems to me that there are two standard methods of 'house training', one being to rub the poor little mite's nose in what it has done, the other to smack it with a folded newspaper. It is hard to say which is the more horrible. Young animals cannot go for any great length of time without emptying both bowels and bladder, yet mothers will wrap their own child up in a nappy and wallop a puppy for behaving like a baby!

Success in house training depends on attention to the following: (1) Practically any puppy brought up under clean conditions *wants* to be clean and it is up to you to allow it to develop this instinct; (2) No eight-weeks-old puppy can go more than a few hours without relieving itself; (3) Regularity in feeding and exercising produces regularity in the working of the puppy's inside; (4) Attentiveness and powers of observation on the part of the owner are essential.

As soon as a puppy settles down, it usually decides on a certain spot where it always goes to relieve itself. It is up to you to see that this is out in the garden or wherever you want it to be. A clean puppy, when it wants to relieve itself, will give some consideration to the place it uses. Although it may not 'ask' to go out by whimpering, the symptoms that it wants to do so should be obvious. When these symptoms appear, take the puppy out, quietly and without fuss, and wait till he does what he should do. Note that I say *take* him out. All too often, the puppy is pushed out, the door shut, and it sits on the step waiting for the door to open. It then comes back in and does what it wants to do where it originally intended doing it.

Many house-training problems arise from the fact that the puppy which has been taken out, comes in, and straight away does indoors what it should have done outside. If it always goes to the same spot, the instinct to be clean is strong; the trouble is it has got things the wrong way round. Several things can be done without resorting to punishment. You can take it out for its usual walk, bring it in and, before it has had time to do anything, take it out again. If it always uses the same mat, remove the mat. You can alter feeding or exercising times— anything which breaks the routine may break this habit.

A useful tip to get a puppy to empty his bowels immediately is to insert a matchstick in the anus in exactly the same way as you would insert a thermometer; let the puppy go and he will immediately get rid of it and everything else. Very soon it gets into the habit of relieving itself immediately it is let out. This method is most helpful with puppies that persist in waiting until they are indoors.

Here we come to another advantage of a playpen. If, when you leave the puppy for the night or at any other time, you put some newspaper down in his pen, it is easy to pick up if he happens to soil it. I am not suggesting that you encourage the puppy to regard his pen as a lavatory, although that is preferable to his using the whole house as one! If he gets into the habit of relieving himself on newspaper, he will, when there is none there, look for it, giving you the opportunity to pick him up and take him out.

Perhaps the most important point of all in house training is regular feeding and exercising. This is not a book on feeding, but I must here make some reference to it and I am afraid I shall contradict a good deal of what has been written on the subject. It is generally agreed that little and often should be the maxim in feeding puppies, with as short a gap as possible between the last feed at night and the first in the morning. In theory that is all very well but, in practice, it causes a great deal of trouble. To give a puppy a large bowl of milk last thing at night and be surprised to find an equally large pool on the floor in the morning is surely ridiculous.

At one time my puppies were fed on orthodox lines, six times a day, then five, then four and so on, and everyone commented on their wonderful condition. For many years, however, they have never had more than four meals a day. By eight weeks they are on to three, with the last at 7 p.m. and the first at 7 a.m., and people still comment on their wonderful condition. By the time they are about six months (depending on weather, how they are doing, etc.) they have only two meals a day, at 7 a.m. and 5 p.m., and it is seldom indeed that a puppy of that age is not perfectly clean in its kennel and run. These dogs are never house trained in the generally accepted sense; they are simply fed and exercised regularly and their own instinct to be clean does the rest.

Naturally the strength of this instinct varies considerably and may, in rare cases, be absent altogether. Quite often it is considerably weakened by a puppy having been reared under filthy conditions. If you have been unfortunate enough to acquire such a puppy, the above methods will not work; you will have to resort to corrective methods. This should never be done until the puppy has gained confidence in you and until you are quite sure that the above method is having no effect.

We must now return to association of ideas, our object being

to make the puppy associate mistakes indoors with an unpleasant experience. The success of all corrective training, whether
applied to the dirty puppy who knows no better or to a deliberately disobedient adult, lies in catching him in the act.
I have, on occasions, waited for days and weeks for an opportunity to catch a dog as he was actually doing what he should
not do (e.g. chasing bikes or rabbits), but, by making full use
of that opportunity, have often cured the dog in *one* lesson.

That is not likely to happen with a young puppy (sometimes
it does); the difficulty arises from the fact that the type of
puppy I am discussing just does what he wants to do wherever
he happens to be. Unlike the puppy whose instinct is to be clean,
this puppy will not trouble to look for any particular spot and,
therefore, gives no warning. The only thing to do is to keep a
constant eye on him, and, when he does squat, grab him by the
scruff, show him what he has done, give him a shake and put
him out. If you catch him in time he will not have done anything and will probably do it outside, when you should praise
him. If you are quick enough to catch a puppy once or twice he
will soon become apprehensive when he feels uncomfortable.
If you are observant, this will be obvious and you can *take* him
out. From then on you can proceed as already advised.

Learning Its Name and Coming When Called

Two things you should teach your puppy right from the
start—its name and to come to you when you call it. Despite
the thought and argument that may have gone into the choice
of a name, to the puppy itself that name is merely a sound.
Now any animal, wild or tame, will go to or run from a particular sound which it associates with pleasure or displeasure
as the case may be. It is a common practice to call poultry,
cattle, sheep and pigs to feed, and many dog owners would be
overjoyed if their dog would come running to them at the pace
hens do in response to the 'cluck-cluck' of the poultryman. The
words matter not, however; cattle and sheep which are in the
habit of having their food carted to them by tractor will run
to the sound of the engine, which cannot be due to any instinct
for there is nothing natural about a tractor. They associate
a certain sound with food, and to show how strongly and how
early this develops I will mention what I have observed in

connection with our own goats. Kids, lambs and other young animals will run to the call of their *own* mother within a few hours of birth. To avoid unnecessary fretting later on, we take our kids from their dams as soon as they are born and hand-feed them. These pay no attention to the bleat of their mother, or any other goat, but within a day or two will run, yelling gleefully, to the voice of the person who feeds them—the sound associated with food.

As soon as they start feeding (at three to four weeks) puppies will come tumbling out of bed in response to 'Puppy-puppy!', a whistle, the rattle of a dish, or whatever sound is associated with food. They will respond to several sounds, but as your puppy will have to learn to differentiate between sounds in the form of words of command, these should, from the start, be as few and simple as possible. Make up your mind, therefore, what you are going to call him and call him *only* by that name. You must use that nice, friendly tone of voice to which I have already referred (*whether you feel like it or not!*), and when he does come you must praise and reward him. At this stage food is probably the best reward you can offer.

Treated in this way, we might expect puppies to come running like hens or like those in Plate IV [a]. That they do not is usually due to the owner, and we might, therefore, take an example to show why one of the commonest of all problems is the dog which refuses to come when called.

Mr. B. and his family have had Rover for about a month, during which time they have shown every consideration in getting the puppy to settle down and become attached to them. It is now decided that Rover, hitherto able to take ample exercise in the garden, might start going for walks. To get to the park, Mr. B. has to walk half a mile through traffic and he has, therefore, given Rover a few lessons on going on a collar and lead. Rover hates the things and he has never been in traffic, which frightens him. However, with the aid of some coaxing, and, no doubt, a little bit of pulling, Rover and Mr. B. eventually arrive at the park, where the puppy is released.

Off he goes to investigate this big new world while Mr. B. strolls along nearby. Rover romps around until Mr. B. decides to go home and moves towards the park exit. When he gets near it he calls Rover, who, on hearing his name, bounces up

PLATE IX

(*a*) Heel work. Note lead hanging slack –
right hand ready to correct the dog, left
hand patting the thigh to encourage him
to come closer
(*Sally Anne Thompson*)

(*b*) Check cord. Note the wooden toggle in right hand

PLATE X

(a) First method

'SIT'

(b) Second method

to Mr. B. as he always has done. Then what happens? That horrid collar and lead is put on again and the puppy taken through that awful traffic.

Next day less trouble is experienced in getting Rover *to* the park, but when it is time to go home, and Mr. B. calls him, he starts off towards him, then halts, and one can almost read his thoughts: 'That horrid lead—that awful traffic! I'm off!'

By the following day Rover has only to see Mr. B. going towards the park exit and he dashes in the opposite direction. So it goes from bad to worse.

'But,' you say, 'he must get the puppy home, there is no way other than through the traffic and he must put him on a lead.' A snag, true, but Mr. B. could have done a great deal to reduce it. First of all, instead of just strolling along he could have frequently called Rover to him, rewarded him and let him go. He could even have put the lead on once or twice, walked a few steps, then taken it off to show the puppy that going on the lead does not necessarily end unpleasantly.

You may think that if Mr. B. calls Rover and rewards him nine times, then provides rather an unpleasant experience on the tenth, it is the last the puppy will associate with the lead. In theory that is what should happen, but in practice it rarely does. One is fairly safe in saying that if you call a puppy ten times, providing pleasure nine times and displeasure once, the chances are nine to one that the puppy will come any time you call him. The chances are likely to increase in proportion to the number of times you reward the puppy when he answers his name. Therefore call him often, reward him lavishly and let him go to enjoy himself.

Mr. B. might have been able to help still further by making the homeward journey less of an ordeal. The reason Rover goes *to* the park so much more willingly each day is that, even on a lead, he soon associates that direction with pleasure, but he expects no such pleasure in going home. If the walk to the park is arranged to coincide with meal-time, on arrival home the puppy will have something to look forward to—a greedy one may even become keener to get home than to go out! A warm welcome on arriving home by any member of the family will give pleasure to any normal puppy.

I

Mr. B. could, of course, have made matters considerably worse either by chasing Rover or by giving him a hiding when he did catch him.

Imagine now a mischievous puppy called in a friendly tone. He comes towards you for a bit, then halts, squats on his elbows, eyes beaming and tail wagging. Make the slightest move towards him and he's off! Run after him and that is terrific fun! Just what he wants, in fact. Ignore him, however, by walking in the opposite direction and that is no fun at all. The chances are that he will come trotting after you; rather disappointed, perhaps, but that is much better from your point of view.

Of course you cannot catch a puppy to put a lead on if you just keep walking in the opposite direction, and we will imagine that you have one which has just started to get into this awkward habit. You call him, he comes so far but no farther, and seems to say, 'Come on, chase me!' *Never* chase a puppy. You can't catch it, anyhow! Instead, sit or squat on your heels and *ignore* the puppy. Puppies appear unable to resist the temptation to investigate, and, if you do that the first time your puppy halts and wants to play, it is almost certain that it will come and put its paws on your knee, when, of course, it should be well rewarded.

If, however, it has had one or two games with you it is unlikely that it will come right up. It will come closer but not near enough for you to touch him. Without looking him in the face, and without moving your body, extend one hand towards him (as in Plate V), at the same time talking to him in a nice friendly, persuasive tone. I realize how difficult that is if you know that you are missing a bus, but it will be quicker in the end and save endless trouble in the future. If you don't move towards him he will, in time, move towards you. As he does so, put some enthusiasm into your voice to try to encourage him further but don't move anything except your fingers. Without training, most dogs will come up to a friendly hand extended towards them with fingers moving. Eventually the puppy will come up to sniff or lick your fingers, when the natural temptation is to grab the little blighter when he is within range! If you succeed in catching him this time, which is unlikely, you certainly won't catch him next time. Instead, withdraw your hand gently, at the same time coaxing him to come with it. As he comes nearer you will be able to stroke his head and cheeks gently. At the same time gradually draw the hand away from the puppy and he should follow it, eventually ending up close beside you. Then, and not until then, reward him by making a great fuss of him and giving him some food and let him go.

'Let him go?' you protest. A natural reaction, but remember that, unless you get him out of this habit, it will almost certainly get worse and you will have even more trouble every time you want to catch your puppy. So let him go, give him a few minutes' freedom, call his name, squat down, as before, and you may be surprised to find that he comes straight up and sticks his little cold nose into the palm of your hand. He may not do this first time but he should be better each time you repeat the performance. Very soon he should, on hearing his name, come straight up to you in anticipation of the reward which you must never forget to give him.

If at any time your puppy is coming to you of his own accord, call him by name and praise him well when he reaches you, but *never* call him when you know perfectly well that he will not answer anyhow. Every time you give a command which is obeyed you have gone a step up the training ladder; every time it is disobeyed you have come a step down. 'But,' you say, 'have I to stand like a fool watching my puppy running away and do nothing about it?' The answer is that unless you are an Olympic sprinter there is nothing you *can* do. You can follow him, of course, and if you are lucky he may decide to return to you.

Whatever you do, don't shout the puppy's name. As we proceed with training the uses to which the name may be put increase. At this stage it is only a sound (always used in a very friendly tone) in response to which the puppy comes to you, in anticipation of some reward, and it should be used *for no other purpose.*

A dog's name repeated over and over again, without association with anything in particular, becomes a sound that means nothing. If my dogs are all playing together and I call any one of them, that *one* dog comes to me but the others pay no attention. That is not due to all the other dogs saying to themselves, 'That's old So-and-So being called, I'm not wanted,' it is because only *one* dog has been taught to come to me in response to that name. All the other names mean nothing, they are sounds with no association, and, where a lot of dogs are exercised and worked together, there are so many of these names being constantly repeated that the dogs to which they do not belong ignore them completely. In exactly the same way many dogs are taught to ignore their *own* names by owners who keep repeating them for no reason at all.

While teaching your puppy his name you should also teach him to associate a certain sound with praise, so that eventually you will be able to praise him at a distance. Every time the puppy comes in response to his name make a great fuss of him. As you do so repeat in a *very* friendly tone, 'Good dog,' 'Good boy,' 'Good girl,' or whatever you fancy. Very soon your puppy, on hearing this sound, will realize that he has done the right thing. By associating a particular word of praise with reward a trained dog will, on hearing it, show obvious pleasure. It is then possible to reward him by voice only. The value of this you will see as we go along.

You may be saying to yourself, 'That's all very well, but I have done all that and, when I call my puppy, he just con-tinues to do what he was doing.' That is the independent 'pack leader' type, and as training depends on balance between correction and reward, when reward fails correction must be applied. Requests are replaced by orders.

The difficulty here is the distance between yourself and the puppy. This can be got over by either of two methods, the safest, although slower, being the check cord method used generally by gundog trainers. Assuming that your puppy is accustomed to collar and lead, put him on a chain slip collar to which is attached about 30 feet of light cord strong enough, but not unnecessarily heavy, for a puppy his size (nylon cord is ideal). Now take him to a place where the cord will not become entangled and let him run 'free' until he is about 20–25 feet away. When you feel certain that he will *not* pay attention, call his name in a friendly tone. Nothing happens! Now change your tone and repeat his name as an *order*. Still nothing happens! Don't wait until it does—follow the command with a sharp jerk on the check cord, remembering that you cannot jerk a cord that is already tight, nor can you time a jerk accurately if you first of all have to coil up a lot of loose cord. This will attract the puppy's attention, when you should repeat his name in a friendly tone. There is a possibility that he will now come right up to you. If he stops, repeat the command in a firm tone and, if necessary, follow it with another jerk, again followed by coaxing in a friendly tone. And don't forget to praise well when the puppy does eventually reach you.

The object is to get the puppy to associate this firm command with correction (a jerk), in anticipation of which he will soon move towards you *before* you apply the jerk. You must, therefore, give him the opportunity to do so. Give the command, wait a second or two; if it is ignored jerk the cord, but if it is answered change the tone of voice completely and call the puppy in a very friendly tone. Don't wait all day—obedience means that a dog should do what it is told *when* it is told. Remember that the check cord is merely a means of communication, enabling you to apply correction at a distance. To simply drag a puppy to you on the end of a cord will do more harm than good.

The other method of correction at a distance (one I usually use myself) requires much more skill and is more likely to go wrong. In it I bridge the gap between myself and puppy without any 'communication cord' by throwing something at him. Imagine that your puppy is investigating a most interesting smell about five or six feet from you. You call him in a friendly tone, knowing quite well that nothing will happen. You repeat his name in a firm tone but this time, instead of a jerk on the collar, something descends upon him from Heaven. What this is depends on circumstances, but if you are out for a walk it is likely you will be carrying a lead, which, when crumpled up in the hand, makes a suitable 'weapon'. In the garden a handful of loose earth gives marvellous results and its spreading effect is helpful to those whose aim is not all it might be! This will give the puppy a fright and he will run for protection—to you —when you must praise and console him. Next time he hears his name in the same tone he will, in anticipation of a similar experience, rush to you in order to escape.

Although this is the best method I know of getting a dog to come when called, it is much more liable to go wrong than the check cord method, when it may well have the opposite to the desired effect. For instance, the puppy must not realize that you threw anything at him or he will, quite naturally, run away from you, not to you. It is possible, however, that, as you are about to throw something, he looks round—he may even decide to come to you after all. It is not everyone who has the alertness of mind necessary to change their tactics instantly and completely to reward instead of correction.

Neither of the above methods of correction is dependent on the infliction of pain. As I have said, dogs are particularly insensitive to physical pain, and shock tactics working on the mind provide quicker and more lasting results. They should, however, be used only on dogs with stable minds. Ideal for the strong-willed puppy, they are *quite unsuitable* for a very young or rather timid one.

If you want to use a word of command such as 'come' in conjunction with the dog's name, there is no harm in doing so provided you always use the *same* word in the right tone. A dog will also answer the sound of a whistle just as readily as the sound of the voice, and it has the advantage that it will carry further.

CHEWING

One habit of which practically all puppies have to be broken is indiscriminate chewing. As with all bad habits, the first step to either cure or prevention is to find out why the dog does it. This is easy in the case of chewing, which puppies do firstly in response to the instinct to catch hold and worry something, and secondly because it is Nature's way of getting rid of the baby milk teeth. For that reason this habit usually develops during teething, and it is for the same reason that you should not try to prevent chewing but merely to prevent chewing the house to pieces.

It is no good, however, just saying, 'Oh, he'll get over it when he has finished teething,' because he may not. The instinct to worry may be diverted to furniture, carpets, etc., and may become so strong that the dog is a constant source of trouble for the rest of his life.

Prevention is the best line of attack. When you cannot keep an eye on him, put your puppy in his pen and give him something to chew. There is quite a selection of toys on the market. Some of the rubber ones are easily broken up and swallowed, making them extremely dangerous. Nylon 'bones' gradually disappear with chewing but they don't break up. Most dogs love 'Chewsticks' which being made of specially prepared rawhide do no harm if eaten. Having given him something to chew, you must now teach him that everything else in the house is taboo. You must be consistent; it is no use saying today, 'Never mind, that's an old pair of stockings,' then beat the poor little brat tomorrow because he treats your best nylons in the same way.

The lessons your puppy is going to have should serve two important purposes. They should teach him to associate chewing anything other than his toy with correction, and they should teach him to associate a certain sound with that correction—to learn that when you say 'No' you *mean* 'No'.

As soon as he begins to feel at home, practically all puppies will find it great fun to seize anything that affords a good grip. Don't try to pull it away—that's just what the puppy wants. Take hold of the puppy (not the object) firmly but gently by the scruff in one hand (*see* Plate VI [a]) and in a firm tone say 'No', at the same time giving him a slight shake (this is just a tightening of the grip rather than a shaking proper). It is sufficient to make a sensitive puppy release its grip, but some tough ones will grip all the tighter in case they lose the object. In that case repeat 'No' in a harsher tone than before (don't shout), following it with a firmer shake. At the same time give the puppy a light tap on the nose with the other hand—with one finger to start with. If that has no effect repeat the process, each time shaking and tapping harder until the puppy releases its hold.

You may think that will make the puppy afraid of your hand and, unless you are careful, it will. There is no need for that to happen, however, if *immediately* the puppy releases his hold you change your whole tactics completely. Keep hold of him, but change the tone of voice from one of scolding to one of praise and, instead of 'No', tell him he is a 'Good dog' (and say it as though you mean it). Most important of all, the hand which corrected him for chewing by tapping his nose must now reward him for letting go by stroking and fondling, the object being to get it firmly established in the puppy's mind that, so long as he does right, you will *never* harm him.

By the time you have done this several times you should find that, when you say 'No' in a scolding tone, the puppy will let go, or at least falter in his game. If he lets go you must tell him he is a 'Good boy' in a praising tone of voice. If he only falters and you praise him *at the right psychological moment* he will let go altogether. If you miss the right moment you may be praising him, not for letting go, but for holding on.

Gradually you should reach the stage where, if the puppy decides to chew the carpet at the other side of the room, all you have to do is say 'No' and he will stop. Likewise you can praise him for obeying. That is one of the most important advances in the whole of the puppy's education. It is the first step towards your being able to apply correction and reward by word of command only. In this way you can tell him whether he is doing the right or wrong thing.

It does not follow that, because a puppy knows what it should and should not do, it will always do what it should. Until they accept the fact that life is very pleasant if they keep out of mischief but equally unpleasant if they do not, most puppies, especially clever ones, will 'try it on' every now and again.

Once a dog knows that it is doing wrong, but only when you are *quite* sure that it knows, you can employ different tactics. In the case of a puppy chewing something which he knows perfectly well he should not chew, shock tactics are probably best. You can dispense with catching the puppy first and simply give him a sudden and *unexpected* rap on the nose with the fingers (see Plate VII [a]). As mentioned earlier, these tactics should be employed *only* on bold puppies, and if perchance you frighten your puppy so that he runs away from you, you *must* make friends with him again *there and then*.

COLLAR AND LEAD

By now I hope your puppy knows his name (and comes when he hears it), that he knows he is doing right when you tell him he is a 'Good dog' and that he is doing wrong when you say 'No'.

Sooner or later you will have to teach him to go on a lead. There is no disadvantage in leaving it until later but the age at which puppies start to go on a lead usually coincides with the age at which they start going out for walks. What age should that be? If you have a reasonable-sized garden, there is no need to take a puppy, even of a big breed, out for the sake of exercise until it is at least four months old.

As I explained in Part I, however, the dog's senses develop as it matures, so that strange people, sounds and sights will have more effect as the puppy gets older. If it is taken out when very young it will grow accustomed to those things and should soon ignore them. Another advantage is that you can easily pick up and carry a little puppy if it panics, whereas an older one must stay on the ground and run the grave risk of being trodden on, which will make it even more afraid.

For these reasons I like to take puppies out as young as possible, the only objection being the risk of disease. Having lost no fewer than forty-one puppies in two outbreaks of Hard Pad, I know how great this risk is and never take a puppy out in public until it has been inoculated. Veterinary surgeons seldom advise this until the puppy is at least three months old*, and as it is not immune for another fortnight that makes it three and a half months, which is older than I like. Although we do not take our puppies in the street or other public place until then, we do try to take them out in the van long before that, often at six weeks. There is no doubt that the earlier they start meeting them, the more easily do they become accustomed to strange experiences, but I must leave it to you to make up your mind according to your own circumstances.

Having made up your mind on this point, you can start teaching your puppy to go on a lead. It is a good idea to have him thoroughly accustomed to this *before* he is taken out, thus avoiding two unpleasant experiences at once—the lead and the traffic. And don't start dragging him around on a lead until he will follow you without one.

Actually no teaching is necessary. All you have to do is let the puppy find out for himself that, when a collar and lead are put on, there is no escape, no matter how much he struggles or how much noise he makes. Let him also find out for himself that to pull on the lead, either forwards or backwards, is decidedly unpleasant, whereas to walk on a loose lead causes no discomfort. If you have by this time developed any sense of

*Consult your own veterinary surgeon for up-to-date advice on inoculation.

'responsiveness' in your puppy, you will be able to add to it by praising well and making the puppy understand that, not only is it much more comfortable for him not to pull, but that he is also pleasing you if he does not do so.

One sometimes finds an improved method of doing something and then, after further experience, decides that the original was better after all. Originally I used an ordinary leather collar to teach a puppy to walk on a lead. Then I decided that a slip collar was more practical. However, having had several puppies which panicked if put into a slip collar straight away, we have gone back to the buckled leather collar to start. After that we decide what is best suited to the individual we are training. The big disadvantage is that some puppies are adept at slipping out of an ordinary collar. Or perhaps I should say that a lot of owners are very bad at preventing this. Always keep the lead under the puppy's chin as in Plate IV [*b*]. If you get it over the top of his head you will pull the collar over his ears whenever he pulls back.

Take your puppy to a place where there is sufficient room and where he is not likely to become mixed up with trees, clothes, poles, etc. Put on the collar and a long, strong lead. Move a bit, to let him discover that he has a collar and lead on. If you are lucky, he will fight it out there and then, doing everything possible to get away. All you have to do is to stand still and hold on, turning round if necessary to avoid becoming a sort of human maypole, and very soon the puppy should stop struggling. Then you must praise him reassuringly to impress on him that *you* do not want to do him any harm, and that he is only hurting *himself*.

If you walk on now, the puppy will probably come with you in stops and starts. When he comes anywhere near where you want him to be, try to stroke and praise him well in a reassuring tone of voice, and the stops and starts should gradually decrease until he is trotting along reasonably well and quite happily. Some puppies will put up several really good fights before giving in, but this type is usually the quickest and easiest to get to go on a lead.

The other type is not nearly so easy—the puppy which, on realizing that he is held, simply sits or lies down and 'says', 'No, I won't.' You can start by coaxing, either with tit-bits or other rewards. But if all else fails, you will just have to reply to his 'No, I won't' with 'Yes, you will,' and, holding the lead behind you, walk on. Soon (usually within a few feet) the friction on the ground will cause some discomfort to the puppy's feet and he will get up to walk a few steps. *Immediately* he does so, or shows the slightest inclination to do so, praise him well, making a great fuss of him, and then continue as before. With a really stubborn puppy this may go on for some time but if you don't give in, he will; and he will decide once and for all that it is much less trouble, and much more comfortable, to walk than be dragged.

Having got him to go on the lead, you now want him to enjoy going on it, and here the essential is to get him to associate the lead with something he enjoys. As an example, when you take him for a romp, take him the first few hundred yards on the lead and then let him go. Soon he will regard the lead as a means of having a jolly good time and will be only too eager to go on it. He may even become too eager, and start to pull, when the answer is not to pull him. Every time he pulls, jerk him back, harder and harder, till he stops it. If you never let pulling become a habit heelwork exercises (page 146) may never be necessary.

Being Left Alone

We now come to some of the problems which may or may not crop up. One which could often be avoided, or at least nipped in the bud, is the dog which creates pandemonium the moment it is left on its own.

Many dogs which hate being left alone do so, not through devotion to their owners, as the latter often believe, but simply through fear. They do not want to protect their owners as a real dog should, they simply want the owner to protect them, to stay and hold their hands as it were! There are, however, many dogs with perfectly good temperaments which cannot be left alone anywhere.

A puppy accustomed from the start to being left in a play-pen *from which it cannot escape* rarely presents this trouble. The usual mistake made is that the moment it squeaks some kind-hearted person lifts it out to console it—in other words, rewards it for making a noise. Of course you do not want to scold a little puppy, but if it does happen to be whining in its pen wait until it is quiet before lifting it out.

If you have a puppy of a big breed an indoor pen will not keep him in for long, but you can tie him up. It is not a big job to put a screw eye in a corner of the kitchen to which about three feet of chain with spring hook is attached. If his bed is kept by it, he can be slipped on to his chain any time he is likely to get in the way or when you go out and leave him. This process can be extended and the puppy fastened to a peg if you happen to be working in the garden. If you give him your jacket or something else to lie on, it will help to develop his guarding instinct and, if he is a real dog, you will probably find that, without any training at all, he will refuse to let a stranger pick it up like the Corgi in Plate XIV [a].

By getting the puppy accustomed to staying in his pen or tied up in the house or garden, you will very soon teach him that there is no escape—when you say he stays *he stays*. He will also learn that, although you leave him quite often, you always come back and, provided he has been good, you praise him. Once a dog realizes that, he rarely presents any trouble when left on his own.

There are, however, some dogs which persist in barking, howling and/or scratching at the door whenever they are shut up. I shall, therefore, describe how I deal with a dog that does this in his kennel and you can adapt the method to suit your own particular circumstances.

I put the dog in the kennel, shut the door and walk a short distance away in a direction that he cannot see me. I then stop and stand quite still until the dog starts barking. Having waited until he has really got going I move stealthily back to the kennel, halting every time he stops barking to prevent his hearing me. When I get right to the door I wait until he is making as much noise as possible, then suddenly whip open the door, grab him by the scruff and give him a thorough shaking to the harsh tone of 'Quiet'. I then close the door and start all over again and, if he starts barking, I repeat the process even more severely each time until he gives it up.

It is very rarely, however, that I have to repeat it immediately, in which case I wait a few minutes, then go back to the kennel in the usual way and praise the dog very well. Probably

I take him out for a walk to reassure him that, so long as he does not bark in his kennel, he and I are the best of friends. Very soon, if he starts barking, all I have to do is shout 'Quiet' and he stops.

Returning to my reference to tying a dog up, it is often argued that to chain a dog makes it bad-tempered, and it is a fact that many bad-tempered dogs may be seen tied up. That, however, is not what breaks their temper. Lack of exercise, furstration due to lack of anything to occupy an active mind, or teasing are the usual causes. A dog shut up in a kennel and run in the same circumstances would become just as vicious.

Which brings us to the question: should a dog kept as a guard rather than a companion live indoors or out? The answer depends on personal circumstances. I was brought up on the idea, still general among working-dog men, that a working dog should never be petted by anyone and should certainly never be allowed indoors. That was supposed to make it soft, but since studying the subject carefully for myself I have come to the conclusion that the idea is a myth. The more a dog is with a person the better the understanding between them. The Metropolitan Police dogs go home with their handlers, where their off-duty life is very much that of any London pet dog.

Nevertheless, a dog may be happier if kept out of doors in a kennel. In many households a dog is wanted and liked by one person but merely tolerated, or perhaps disliked, by another. There is no doubt that such a dog is far happier outside on his own than left alone with the latter person.

If you do decide to keep a dog out of doors, there are certain points to note. He must have a weatherproof house, raised off the ground with the sleeping bench placed round the corner from the entrance, so that the wind does not blow straight in.

If you use a chain it should be as strong as, but no heavier than, necessary. The 'weak link' in most chains is the spring hook and swivel. Many dogs are weighed down by a chain that would hold a horse, fastened to their collar by a hook that would not hold a cat. It is essential that the swivel should turn freely, otherwise the dog can easily wind the chain up until it chokes. Where a dog is left for any length of time it is advisable to have two swivels. When you tie your dog up see that he cannot wind the chain round anything. If you tie him by a wall or fence see that the chain is short enough to prevent his jumping over and hanging himself. A running chain on a wire can be shorter, therefore ligher, and at the same time give the dog more freedom. It also quite often causes less inconvenience for the dog to occupy a long narrow strip on a wire than a large round patch on a long chain. Apart from which he may be in a better strategic position as a guard.

Whether kept in a run, on a chain, or allowed to run in the garden, do try to prevent teasing by passers-by. Dogs hate being stared at, laughed at, or poked at, all of which some people regard as highly amusing. Apart from deliberate teasing, many dog lovers, with the very best intentions, do all those things in an effort to 'make friends'. Although there are many people who love all dogs, there are few dogs that love all people. Many become vicious by teasing of the above nature. The only solution I have been able to find to this problem is to keep your dog out of range of passers-by.

JUMPING UP

Dogs that jump up on their owners or, worse still, on other people, are a common problem. The remedy for the latter is discipline, which means that, if you see the dog rushing towards someone, you simply call it back or give it the command 'Down'. That is not always practicable with the dog that jumps up on its owner, and here, as in everything else, prevention is better than cure. In all training, right from the start, praise a puppy *only* when it is on the ground. If, for instance, when you call it to you it comes with a great rush and jumps up, don't scold it; push it gently off you before praising it. Soon it should learn that jumping up results in nothing, while staying on the ground is rewarded.

If you have a dog that has got into this habit there are two things you can do. The first is to let the dog hurt himself in jumping up. If you have a really boisterous 'jumper-upper' that takes a running leap at you, wait until he is in the air and bring your knee up quickly to catch him in the middle. His own force provides the impact and will probably wind him momentarily. Few dogs like that and there is no risk

of building up a wrong association of ideas—of the dog thinking he is being corrected for coming to you instead of for
jumping up.

Remember that, to you, there is a vast difference between
an eight-weeks-old puppy jumping up to about knee level and
the same dog a year later jumping up round your neck. To the
dog, however, there is no difference, it is still only being as
boisterous and friendly as possible. Having been allowed, or
even encouraged, to do so in the first place, it sees no reason why
it should not continue. It is also unfair to encourage a dog to
jump up in play when you are in your old clothes, then curse
him for doing the same thing when you are dressed.

A second method, employing the same principle, applies
more to the dog that stands up rather than bounces on you.
Simply tread (lightly, of course) on his hind feet, tapping first
on one, then the other, until he goes down, when you should
praise him.

In neither case is a word of command necessary, or even
desirable, as you are not teaching the dog anything. You are
merely providing circumstances through which he should learn
for himself that jumping or standing up is a most uncomfortable
pastime.

PESTERING DOGS

There is nothing more annoying than a dog which pesters
its owner or visitors to the house in the hope of being petted or
given tit-bits. You should not, and I hope would not, punish
a puppy just because it wants to be friendly or because it wants
food. On the other hand, if you pander to it, you will soon find
that you have *two* problems: (1) a dog that is a perfect pest and
never leaves you or your friends alone for a minute, and (2) when
you want to reward it in training you cannot do so, as it has
become accustomed to petting and feeding, both of which it
takes for granted. It is worth noting that many people will eat
far more than is good for them, in spite of the fact that they
are capable of reasoning and know what happens to people
who eat too much. It is not, therefore, surprising that dogs,
which are not capable of reasoning, will, if allowed or encouraged, eat far more than is good for them.

If your puppy pesters you to play games, or just to be petted, the point to remember is that it takes two to make a success of such pastimes. If you won't he can't, and the thing to do is to ignore him. A whole family sitting round a table glancing at the puppy and saying 'Let's pay no attention to him' are *not* ignoring him. By ignoring him I mean ignoring him completely, which he will soon find is no fun at all. An odd piece of food from the table will not turn a dog into an inveterate begger—so long as he has it when *you* offer it and *not* when *he* asks for it.

The same applies to chasing sticks or any other games that may become an obsession. It is not generally realized just how much effect an obsession can have on a dog's mentality. I have seen cases of dogs becoming neurotic and eventually imbecile as a result of being obsessed with something. And I have seen many cases of dogs which were virtually untrainable until an obsession was broken. Any tendency to develop a 'thing' about anything should, therefore, be discouraged or, if necessary, corrected before it has become established.

PLATE XI

(a) 'Sit', third method

(b) 'Down.'

PLATE XII

(b) Teaching the 'down' can be combined with other jobs
(*Sally Anne Thompson*)

(a) Instincts in untrained puppies. Collie 'eyeing' a
Labrador retrieving

CHAPTER IX

TRAINING THE YOUNG DOG

Heel work—The Down—Encouraging and controlling the guarding instinct
—Jealousy—Fighting—Chasing

WE now come to the training your dog is likely to require as
he grows up. This can be divided quite distinctly into two
sections: what I call disciplinary exercises on the one hand, and
the checking of bad habits and the encouragement of good ones
on the other. Disciplinary exercises are designed to make a dog
more responsive, to develop his submissive instinct and, in
short, to make him more obedient. Habits, good and bad,
almost invariably arise from the instincts. This chapter,
therefore, deals with the control of the hunting and guarding
instincts in their various forms.

It should be noted that to encourage an instinct, to develop
something that is there, is quite different from the teaching of
disciplinary exercises, which are almost entirely negative. To
teach a dog to lie down or walk to heel is easy; it is teaching
him not to get up or run off that is difficult. By comparison,
developing an instinct is not really training, but if that instinct
is to be kept under control once it has developed, training is
absolutely essential. For that reason it is of the greatest importance to prevent these instincts developing until the dog is
disciplined, and the age at which they show signs of taking
control may well decide the age at which disciplinary training
should be started.

Disciplinary training I shall confine to the two exercises
which form the basis for the training of Police dogs, for
obedience competition dogs and for the great majority of dogs
sent to professional trainers as 'difficult' or 'disobedient'. These
exercises are known as 'heel work' and the 'down'.

K   145

HEEL WORK

This is usually regarded as the basis of all obedience training, but to show how impossible it is to generalize I might mention that it is never used in the training of working sheepdogs. Who would argue that a better understanding between man and dog can be seen in the obedience ring at Cruft's Dog Show than at the International Sheepdog Trials? Heel work is not the basis of *all* training, but it is probably the best foundation for those who want an obedient dog but have no work for it. It has *two* objects. Firstly, it is the best and quickest method of getting a dog to walk properly to heel, either on a slack lead or without a lead. Its value in this direction is so great that its even greater value in quite another direction is often overlooked. A little heel work is quite the best way I know of making a dog pay attention, thereby making him more submissive or responsive. A dog that has got into the habit of ignoring the commands of his owner will benefit from this exercise no matter how old it is. Both correction and reward are applied and varying tones of voice are used, so that if the dog does not already respond to those 'aids' he can quickly be made to do so. The advantage in that is that, once you get a dog to do something, *anything*, on command, the easier does it become to teach him something else.

Young puppies should never be given heel-work exercises; these should be left until the character has developed and the dog begins to show that it has a mind of its own. The age at which that happens varies so much that it is almost impossible to offer guidance. I have known six-month-old puppies which really needed discipline and two-year-old dogs far too 'puppyish' to stand up to it.

If you have a dog that follows to heel, is obedient and responsive, there is no need to teach this exercise, and any attempt to do so may result in it becoming thoroughly 'fed up' with the whole business. Neither is it necessary to keep on practising these disciplinary exercises once the dog knows them. There is nothing a trained dog enjoys more than being put through his paces, but dogs, like us, can have too much of a good thing, and there is nothing so boring as constant repetition. You need not worry lest your dog forgets, as dogs never forget anything they really know.

It is customary in modern training to teach the dog to walk

on the left side; this is compulsory in obedience competitions and Police Dog Trials. The reason is that, being on the left side, the Police or Service dog leaves the handler's right (armed) hand free. Since taking up film work we have had no difficulty in teaching all our dogs to walk on either side. For practical purposes this is often quite an advantage, but in writing about it I will assume that the dog is always on your left side.

In general use for modern obedience training is the chain slip collar which is simply a piece of chain with a ring either end. The chain is passed through one of the rings and the lead attached to the other. This slip collar, also known by the misleading name of choke collar, is regarded by some as an instrument of cruelty, and by others as a magic device to stop a dog pulling. There is no collar which stops a dog pulling. Like a bit in a horse it merely enables the trainer to keep the animal under control—if he knows how to use it! Whether it is cruel or not depends on the trainer, not the collar.

To put on a slip collar stand facing the dog as in Plate VIII [a]. With the ring to which the lead is attached held in the left hand slip the collar over the dog's head. This means that the running ring on the collar comes up on the right side of the neck when tightened and immediately falls down when slackened. If put on the wrong way round the ring will be pulled up the left side and over the back of the neck; here it will remain when the lead is slackened.

Although the slip collar is still used generally in obedience training circles, we have changed to the more modern double-action collar.

Instead of the single chain with ring either end, we have two chains, one exactly the same as an ordinary slip collar. The other is a shorter, endless chain passing through the two rings on the ends of the first and also through a free ring to which the lead is attached as in Plate VIII [c].

We started using it because so often when a film artist has to lead a dog, he or she either allows it to slip an ordinary leather collar or strangles the poor brute on a single-action slip! Neither of these things can happen with a correctly fitted double-action. The only disadvantage is that, whereas an inch either way makes very little difference in fitting the ordinary slip collar, to be effective the double-action collar must fit the dog exactly.

In the first picture we have a collar long enough to go right round the dog's neck but not any longer. When pulled up as in the illustration this will neither slip over the dog's head nor will it run tight. Sensative dogs which resent the ordinary slip collar do not usually resent this at all.

With an insensitive dog you can use a shorter collar as in the second picture (this is just long enough to go over the dog's head) which can be jerked up tight to give just as severe correction as the ordinary slip collar.

In both cases the collar, when not in action, hangs comfortably round the base of the neck. And it cannot be put on the wrong way round. The action is exactly the same whether the lead is held in the left hand or the right. Although I invariably teach heel work on the left I have found there are occasions when it is a great help if a dog will be led on the right. Also, in spite of all the instructions in books, on T.V. and at training classes about fifty per cent of the dogs I see wearing orthodox slip collars have them on the wrong way round!

Having got the collar comfortably on the dog, stand facing in the same direction, the dog on your left side. The lead should be at least three feet long, strong, light and pliable. Hold this in your right hand, with your elbow bent at a right angle, and allow the loop where the lead bends to hang about half-way between the dog's neck and the ground. And get it fixed in your mind that the right hand is the correcting hand, the left the rewarding one.

Now move off quickly, saying the dog's name, followed by a sharp 'Heel'. It is unlikely that the dog will move as quickly, so you give him a little, quick jerk with the right hand. This should bring him up to you, when you must immediately reward him by caressing and fussing with the left hand. This is easy with a big dog whose head is about level with your hand but not so easy with a little one. If the dog rushes forward on the lead, let him go and, at the instant when he is about to reach the end, turn sharp right, at the same time jerking with the right hand so that (in the case of a big, strong dog) you have his own strength combined with yours in the jerk. Keep on turning right, both at right angles and right about, jerking him to you every time he wanders the wrong way. Never forget to praise and encourage with the left hand. Pat your thigh, stroke his cheek with your fingers—do anything that you find will get him closer to you.

The top picture in Plate IX was taken a split second after the dog had been corrected for pulling ahead. Note the lead slack and the left hand extended to praise the dog as he comes up in response to the correction.

In obstinate cases you can occasionally turn left and 'crash' into the dog, but too much of this will tend to keep him away from you instead of bringing him closer. Make all your movements quick and 'alive' and keep turning in different directions, so that the dog will not know which way you will turn next. Never work to a set plan; as well as getting the dog to keep close to you, you are trying to get him to concentrate on your actions. This he should do when he realizes that every time his mind wanders, he receives a sharp jerk, but that he will be praised and fussed when he pays attention.

The degree of jerking necessary varies considerably from dog to dog. A terrific jerk on a slip collar to a thin-skinned, sensitive dog like a Greyhound would amount to downright cruelty and the dog would probably go to pieces. On the other hand, a little jerk would not be felt at all by a big powerful young Alsatian, which had been pulling its owner all over the place since it was three months old. With a big strong dog a good deal of physical strength is necessary in the initial stages, and that is one reason why many owners, particularly ladies, put in a lot of hard work with no result.

Incidentally, this is one exercise in which I have found that rewarding with food does no permanent good, and may even do harm. It will get a dog to keep up with you so long as you have food in your hand, but one cannot go around constantly offering pieces of meat.

In teaching heel work it is usual to train the dog to sit automatically every time the trainer halts. This looks smart and has the practical advantage that it is much easier to teach a dog to sit still than to stand still. If you stop to speak to a friend or at the kerb you do not want your dog wandering ahead, the easiest and best way to avoid this is to teach him to sit automatically.

There are several ways of making a dog sit (it is not usually very difficult) but I generally use either of two. As soon as the dog is walking freely on a loose lead and coming up close to you in response to your left ('rewarding') hand, stop suddenly, at the same time giving the command 'Sit', swing your body round to the left (not moving your feet) and move the right hand over the dog's head as in Plate X [a]. About fifty per cent of dogs will look up to your right hand and, when your movements are combined with a sudden halt, will go down on their haunches. The whole thing must be carried out simultaneously from a walk. It is no good stopping and then moving your right hand in the hope that the dog will sit; it must be done *as you halt*.

You may, however, have the kind of dog which just stands and looks at you as though you had gone a bit 'odd'. In this case you will have to force him into a sitting position by pulling back on the collar with the right hand, at the same time pressing on his rump with the left. In Plate X [b] the right hand is held high as this dog has a tendency to lie down. Most dogs are inclined to lean forward and it is likely that you will have to hold your hand lower and farther back to enable you to pull the dog back on to his haunches. See that he sits square on his haunches or on his right side, which brings him towards you.

The first method is less laborious; I always try it first, and if it fails, go on to the second. Whichever you adopt, be sure to praise your dog very well whenever he sits, and try to get him close to you right from the start. If he sits too far from you, do not move towards him; move to the right, away from him, coax him to you with your left hand but, if necessary, swing his haunches towards you with the same hand as he sits down. Never move towards your dog, except when returning to him after a sit or down. Always make him move towards you.

Do not keep on gently pushing him into a sitting position every time you halt. That will teach him nothing; it will only get him accustomed to your pushing him down. Be gentle to start with, but, if he does not respond, gradually replace the push with the left hand with a slap on the rump. Remember that a dog must not only do what you want, he must do it quickly. A dog that is a bit slow on his sits can often be speeded up by combining the two methods. Stop suddenly, swing the right hand over the dog and, with the tip of the lead which is held in that hand, give him a sharp flick on the rump. Never forget to praise him when he sits, especially the first time he shows the least inclination to sit of his own accord.

To make a dog sit facing me I usually use a different method to that described in teaching a dog to sit to heel. Grip the lead close to the collar under the dog's chin, or put your hand through the collar, as in Plate XI [a]; pull to you and slightly upwards. When the dog is moving, suddenly release the pull and, if nedessary, push backwards on the throat. The latter is rarely necessary as, by releasing the tension quickly, the dog will sit back on his haunches like a person pulling a rope which breaks. Don't forget to give the command 'Sit' as you pull him up and praise him when he does it—even if it is by accident.

Repeat each exercise until you get some sign of response, praise very well, and leave it for the day. Next day you will be able to start where you left off, and so should steadily progress, whereas if you keep on and on, the dog will sooner or later get bored and you may be farther back than when you started. After a while you will find that your dog is sitting smartly each time you halt, although he may sometimes still need an extra command, but practice should soon make that unnecessary.

You should now have a dog doing heel work very nicely on the lead, keeping right up alongside your left leg to receive that little encouragement from your left hand and turning sharply to the right when you turn, to avoid that sharp jerk on the lead if he does not. If he does these things—but not unless—you can try a bit of 'heel free' and here you will find whether or not you have been training him in the right way. If you have, and own the right dog, you will find that he will do his heel work just the same off the lead as on. If you have been jerking at him in a lifeless, mechanical sort of way, without rewarding him at the right time, he will, in all probability, follow well behind or away on your left. In this case slip the lead back on and start again, trying to get him to respond to the left hand, using the right one only when that fails. Remember that when you take the lead off you still have your left (rewarding) hand for encouragement, but your right (correcting) hand is gone.

Quite a number of the 'naughty' type of dogs make a dash for freedom when the lead is removed, even if they have been doing Heel on Lead quite well. Fortunately, they almost invariably rush ahead, and the best and quickest way I have found to stop their rush is as follows: Halt as usual with the dog sitting to heel on the lead, remove the lead and hold both ends in the right hand so that it hangs in a loop by your side, where the dog cannot see it. Next, start off smartly in exactly the same way and with the same commands you have been using. Try to keep him to your left side by encouragement with the hand, but he may walk a few steps and then, without any warning, go off like a shot from a gun. As he does so, not before or after, give him a 'stinger' on the hindquarters with the lead.

This should make him rush back to you for 'protection', whereupon you must praise him very well indeed. No dog, even the very hardest, likes to be hit by something 'out of the blue', but this method has its snags. You have only a split second in which to act, and it will test your ability to anticipate what the dog is going to do. It will also test your ability to praise your dog instantly when he does the right thing. If you do it properly, it is unlikely that you will ever have to do it again. If you miss him and he does not notice that you tried to hit him, you will have done neither good nor harm. But if he sees you make a swipe at him and you miss, you will be farther back than before you started. Do not forget to give a sharp 'Heel' as you go to hit him—so that next time you say 'Heel' as he decides to go he will associate it with that sudden sting which came 'out of the blue' and, instead of running away, he will come closer to you.

Although I think that every dog should be taught to walk to heel properly, I do not think that any dog should ever be taken in traffic without a lead. Dogs, like us, make mistakes, no matter how well they are trained. When, in my late teens, I used to drove sheep to Perth market, I had a really wonderful bitch, Floss, of which I was very proud. When my sheep had been sold I usually went down town and, like many others who like to show off a bit, I never put Floss on a lead. After all, no one had a better dog and certainly no one could train one better than I (so I thought!), and it would be *infra dig.* to put her on a lead.

One day when I was walking down High Street, Floss at heel, two boys came running one after the other down an alley on to the pavement where Floss happened to be. She had either to be run into or get out of the way quickly. In her hurry to get out of the way she rushed straight into the middle of the traffic. She came back almost as quickly as she went—un-harmed—but, from that day, I have never taken a dog in traffic off a lead and never shall. There is no good saying *your* dog would not do that, as I was quite sure that Floss would not do it either—until she did. Your dog may not be so lucky as she was!

Quite apart from the safety to both dog and road-users, a dog on a lead has far more freedom in traffic than one walking close to heel, as it must do, without a lead. Does not a child, of its own free will, take its mother's hand when in a crowd? It then does not worry about getting left behind and its mind is free to enjoy what it sees around it. In exactly the same way a dog, off a lead, has to concentrate on keeping with its owner while one on a lead need not worry. To the owner a dog that walks properly to heel on a slack lead is no more trouble and far less worry than one without a lead.

Considering the number of two-legged 'jay walkers' to be seen everywhere, it surprises me how many people expect dogs to have 'traffic sense' and regard as stupid those which do not. Dogs which have—and there are many—have acquired this sense by an association of ideas, usually by being run into by a car or some other narrow escape from death.

THE DOWN

The second disciplinary exercise is the 'Down', which I consider the most important of all. Obviously a dog lying down cannot bite the postman passing a few feet away, chase the message boy or jump up and leave dirty pawmarks on the best clothes of a special visitor. Even if it will not come when called, a dog that will go down, and stay there until you go to it, is greatly to be preferred to one that runs away. In the working of any dog, the first essential is that it will drop on command. Until it does so it is of little practical value.

Those who have never owned a companion dog that will lie down quietly where and when it is told, and stay there, have rarely any idea how little trouble a trained dog can be. To many people, a dog that is not continually rushing about must be tired. If, however, you go to Whipsnade Zoo you will see wolves in as near natural conditions as most people care to see wolves. But you will not see them rushing around madly like many pet dogs do. They will play together and potter around, but when there is nothing better to do they just lie down and go to sleep, which is the natural thing to do and what any sensible dog will do.

This can be encouraged by teaching the dog to 'Down' until it becomes another good habit. Those dogs which are never still either have restless temperaments or are made that way by owners who never leave them alone. A dog which will lie still to allow people to step over it is far less of a nuisance than one that bobs about all over the place. Apart from that, a sensitive dog, with a tendency to be 'jumpy', can often be steadied by making it lie down and showing it that, if it stays still, no-one will hurt it. Provided of course that no one *does*.

If you intend taking part in obedience competitions you will have to teach your dog the difference between 'Sit' and 'Down', and these should be clearly defined right from the start. There are occasions when a working dog has a better range of vision sitting up, but I have found that, for most practical purposes, it is sufficient to teach the dog to sit on heel work, etc., and to put him down if he is to remain in the same place for any length of time. If you are teaching the 'sit' and 'down' as separate exercises remember that 'Sit' means sit, 'Down' means down, and 'sit down' is a term often used by muddle-headed people whose dogs rarely know what is wanted!

The advice I am about to give refers to teaching either the 'Sit' or the 'Down', the method of teaching either being the same. The most important point is not whether the dog lies down or sits up but that he *stays where he is told to stay*.

When starting any new exercise always choose a quiet spot free from distractions and put the dog on a lead. Now take the lead in your right hand and put your left foot on it so that it can run beneath the instep. Now give the command 'Down' in a firm tone and at the same time pull up with the right hand and push down with the left across the dog's shoulders as in the picture, Plate XI [b]. It is quite often possible to get a dog to lie down through fear by simply threatening him in a harsh tone. Although you do not want to do that, you should make some use of the dog's instinct to crouch down in response to a harsh tone. He will soon learn that, when he does, nothing unpleasant happens.

Having got the dog down by sheer force, sometimes quite a struggle, wait until he relaxes for just a second, then praise him gently. Some trainers disagree about this, maintaining that to praise a dog on the down will immediately make him get up. That is true, but if you promptly change your tone to a firm 'Down' and put him back he will soon realize that he is being rewarded for staying down. By using *both* correction and reward, the dog will go down much more willingly and more pleasantly than by using correction alone.

Once you get the dog on the ground, *keep him there* until he stops struggling. Immediately he does, praise him gently by stroking his head and by tone of voice (but don't make a great fuss of him or he will jump all over you) and let him get up. If you can get him to relax for half a second, praise him and allow him to get up you have gone a step forward. If you struggle for half an hour without getting him to relax you have merely been teaching him to struggle. Repeat this procedure perhaps four or five times in the first lesson and you will be surprised to note how much more easily and willingly he goes down each time.

Having got the dog to lie down, the next thing is to get him to stay there. This can be done by putting your foot on the lead close to his collar and pressing it on the ground. Stand up straight, and if he attempts to get up give him the command 'Down', if necessary pushing him down again. As he cannot get right up he should soon learn that the only comfortable position is lying quietly by your foot.

You have now got the dog lying still beside you but you have not yet taught him to lie down. All you have done is to accustom him to being pushed into position and to stay there because he cannot get up. When he does that without protest you have negotiated the first obstacle; the next is to get him to do it on command, and the usual mistake here is that people never give their dog a chance. They give the dog the command and, before he has had time to obey, they shove him to the floor, thereby teaching him to associate the sound 'Down', not with lying down, but with being pushed down. He, therefore, merely waits to be pushed. When you give the command, wait a second or two, then, if nothing happens, give the lead in the right hand a bit of a tug and give him a push on top of the shoulders—but don't keep up a continuous pressure. If he shows the slightest response, praise him well *as he responds*, and if he falters give him another tug or push. The object is to get the dog to lie down on command in anticipation of the correction which will follow if the command is ignored. That is the second obstacle over.

Now we come to the third obstacle, the one on which most people get stuck—getting the dog to stay in position while you move away. Of the dogs which came to me for training, quite a number would sit smartly or lie down on command, but none would stay there. Why? Because, in spite of tremendous efforts on the part of the owners, the dogs have never been taught to do so. I shall, therefore, try to describe the usual mistakes.

Firstly the dog is made to sit, the trainer stands facing it and, when the dog is sitting nicely, it is called to him and praised for having stayed sitting. At least, that is what those people *think* they have praised the dog for doing. What they have actually done is praise it for coming to them—the very thing they don't want it to do. Add to this the fact that the dog does not want to remain sitting because it wants to go to its master (who has been teaching it to do so since it was a baby), and you may realize why this method produces so many failures. Not only do these people praise the dog for doing what they don't want it to do, they praise it for doing what it *does* want to do.

The second reason for failure is that people order the dog to sit or down, then forget all about it. If it is told to down and gets up of its own accord half an hour later, it has been disobedient—you have gone a step back (often a very big step). If it stays down for half a minute and gets up when *you say so*, you have gone a step forward. If, therefore, you have just made your dog lie down and the 'phone rings, don't go off and leave him. To avoid the risk of his getting up before you return, praise him for having gone down, let him up or put him on a lead and take him with you.

Bearing the above mistakes in mind, let us return to the dog which will now lie down on command beside you and stay there without struggling. The secret of success in this exercise is to make haste slowly. Before you try to get a dog to stay down while you walk away, make sure that he will stay *for a much longer period* beside you. This can be practised in the home while you are doing something else. If, when you are having a meal or reading the papers, you keep him by you with your foot on the lead as in Plate XII [b], a dog will very soon get into the habit (another good habit) of lying quietly beside you.

Once he does that, but not until, you can start teaching him to stay down while you move away. Begin with the dog on a lead, tell him to 'Down' and stand facing him. Now move a step backwards and if he shows signs of getting up, order him to 'Down' *before he does it.* You can use the command 'Stay' now to strengthen your 'Down' and if, every time you left him as a puppy in his pen, or tied up, or simply went out leaving him in the house, you said quietly and firmly 'Stay' instead of 'Be a good boy, darling. Daddy be back soon,' he will now know the meaning of that command. If he stays, move back to him, praise him and move away again.

Now move to one side, then to the other, lead still in hand, and do it all quietly and smoothly. If he stays, praise him again and, still holding the lead, try to move right round the back of him. Here, you may find that he wants to move round with you and you must correct this immediately. Keep the lead on until he will let you walk round the back of him and step over him from either side. In case you are thinking that you don't have time to go through all this, I might mention that I can usually get a dog I have known for about a week to this stage in about ten to fifteen minutes, when I usually end the first lesson.

The next stage is surreptitiously to drop the lead beside the dog, hoping he does not realize that you are no longer holding it. This will enable you to move farther away and gradually increase the distance in all directions. If the dog gets up and comes towards you, don't just shout 'Down' and be content if he obeys. This is one of the few occasions in training when you go towards your dog. Do this quickly and quietly, take him by the collar and with a firm 'No' take him back to the exact spot from which he got up and order him to 'Down' and 'Stay'. So important is this exact spot that I often make a mark when I am training, but don't leave an object which you have handled, otherwise the dog may stay by an object belonging to you but refuse to stay without one.

When the dog will allow you to walk quite some distance away and to walk over him or past him, you should *gradually* increase the length of time you keep him down. Much of this training can be done in the home or when you are working in the garden *so long as you keep your mind on the dog*. Once he will stay in a familiar place you can try him where there are distractions. But don't make the poor brute stay down in the street or in big stores. If I were a busy housewife doing some shopping, my mind would be on what I was looking for, which would certainly not include dogs lying on the pavement!

To teach your dog to stay down while you go out of sight, put it down in the usual way, move some distance away, slip quietly behind a tree or some other object and return almost immediately. Many dogs will get up the moment their trainer goes out of sight for the first time, but if the trainer suddenly reappears to correct this they are taken by surprise and are much less likely to do it next time. Although the dog is unable to see you, you must be able to see him to enable you to correct him if he moves. Gradually increase the length of time you stay out of sight and a dog with a good temperament will soon realize that you are not leaving him for good.

Until your dog is quite reliable in this exercise never call him to you; always go back to him and praise him for having stayed. For practical purposes, of course, a dog is often called up from the down, but this should never be done until he is quite steady. Even then, do not call him every time. If he shows the slightest tendency to get up before you call, put him down again firmly and finish the lesson by going back to praise him. And don't forget that if you are just going to tell him to get up and he gets up before you have done so (even a split second before), he has disobeyed you. Put him down again, just for a second, and make him stay there until *you say* he can get up.

A definite command can be used to let the dog know he is free, but I 'release' my dogs from the down, heel work or any other exercise merely by tone of voice and by adopting the attitude that, as they have been very good, they can now go and enjoy themselves. A bit vague, perhaps, but the dogs soon know.

Having discussed one essential, getting the dog to stay, we now come to another equally important point—getting him to lie down *quickly*. This exercise, dropping on command, can be taught while the dog is also having lessons in staying, so we shall go back to what I described as the second obstacle, getting the dog to lie down on command. If you say 'Down' and the dog goes down, no matter how reluctantly, you know that he has got the meaning of the command, but if you say 'Down' and push him to the floor you have no idea whether or not he understands.

If you are *sure* that he knows the command, you can hurry a slow dog quite considerably, although some dogs present no difficulty and will lie down quickly after one or two lessons. The object is simply to let the dog see that you do not intend waiting all day. You give the command, the dog begins to think about it, so you put your foot firmly on the lead (still held in the right hand, forming a loop below the dog's neck), giving his head a jerk downwards, at the same time repeating the command. Very soon you should find that the dog, in anticipation of this jerk, will lie down quickly, when, of course, you praise him well.

When the dog goes down quickly by you on a lead you can teach him to go down a distance away, off the lead, and, here again, gradually increase the distance. If the dog is sufficiently steady to be called from the down, the best way of teaching this is by practising a 'drop on recall'. Put the dog down, walk some distance away, call him and, as he comes towards you, give him the command 'Down'. If he obeys, go forward and praise him; if he does not, don't stand repeating the order and waiting for him to do so. Go forward to meet him, quietly and quickly, put your hand on the collar under his neck and jerk him down with a severe 'Down'. If he has continued to move towards you after the command, take him back and put him down on the spot where he should have dropped. Once your dog has got the idea you can praise him by tone of voice and there is no need to go up to him. Once he is reliable you can call him up to you again after you have dropped him.

Whatever you do, don't work to a routine in any training. If you always put your dog down, walk so many paces away, call him, drop him half-way, then call him up again; you may produce a brilliant competition dog but one that is of no practical value. Such a dog will probably not drop at all unless that whole procedure is gone through. If you are out for a walk give your dog an unexpected 'Down' when he is coming to you or going away—the object being to get him to drop instantly on command, anywhere, any time. Go to praise him sometimes, call him at other times and avoid any risk of monotony in your dog or yourself. And don't forget that if you tell a dog to lie down you must tell him to get up.

This exercise is one where a hand signal as well as a word of command is of great advantage. I simply point to the ground, making the signal as clear as possible by moving the whole arm downwards. Many trainers use the upraised hand, like a policeman on point duty, which is very clear. My only reason for not using it is that I use it as a signal to stand, dropping the arm as mentioned when I want the dog to go down.

Whatever signal you use, stick to it and use it simultaneously with the word of command. In time the dog should obey the one just as well as the other and, if you want to strengthen the order, you can use both together.

The Guarding Instinct

The guarding instinct is one which you want to develop without risk of over-development. As I have said, few puppies show any inclination to guard until they are at least six months old (often over a year), and those which show a dislike for strangers very early are usually either shy or much too aggressive for your purpose when they mature. Don't forget, either, that a sensible dog guards what *belongs* to him and is unlikely to show much inclination to guard until he settles down in a new home.

Guarding is not, as some people imagine, simply a case of making a noise at the approach of a stranger; the first indication that this instinct is developing may not be barking at all. If, as a stranger approaches, your puppy sits up and takes note, perhaps with a bit of a growl, encourage him immediately. By now he should understand praising by tone of voice alone, but remember that tone of voice can do more than correct or reward a dog—it can calm an excitable dog or excite a placid one. If your young dog shows no great interest in strangers you can 'egg him on' by saying 'Who's that?' or something in an exciting tone. Do not, however, forget that the object is to get the dog to bark at the sound of a stranger, and the dog which barks only when you say 'Who's that?' is little better than one that does not bark at all. And don't 'cry wolf' when there is no one there.

When someone comes to the door let him run to it and encourage him to bark before you open it, but this is necessary only in the case of a dog with a rather weak guarding instinct. Most dogs will, if allowed, do that without encouragement, but many people who want a dog to guard will, if it happens to bark when they are in conversation or listening to the radio, curse and even beat it. In the case of a puppy with only a normal guarding instinct, this procedure is like trampling on a newly planted seedling which, with a little encouragement, could so easily grow into a strong and useful plant.

A far more common problem is the guarding instinct that threatens to get out of control. This takes several forms, perhaps the most aggravating of which is evident if one tries to carry on a conversation in a doorway with a lady struggling to hold a big young dog that is barking its head off. Here both our disciplinary exercises can be put into practice. If the dog will stay to heel on command there will be no need to hang on to him, but the essential thing is that he can be put down quickly, and that he will *stay* there. Obviously, a dog lying in the doorway cannot bite someone standing on the step, but of even greater importance is the fact that no one standing on the step is likely to give him the chance! I have tried to illustrate the importance of this strategic position by staging two photographs (Plate XIII). In one Tazzi is barking behind a 'caller', in the other she is lying silently in the doorway. As it happens, this Bearded Collie is police-trained and is a 'hot' natural guard. To describe as slender the chances of any stranger molesting the lady in the doorway would be a gross understatement, even if she were behind him. If, however, she were untrained it is possible that she could be taken off her guard and the man could be inside with the door closed before she realized what was happening. This would be only too easy if she were any farther away than in the picture.

Another advantage in this strategic position is that people, especially evil-doers, tend much more readily to move away from the danger that is behind them than towards the danger that stares them in the face. Which brings us to another important point: if you have a dog which is in fact friendly with

L

everybody and you train it to lie down as described, it will look the part. Furthermore, by teaching a friendly dog to lie quietly by the door it is probable that it will gradually realize that it does not go there to have a rollicking time. It goes for a purpose and there is every possibility that the guarding instinct will gradually develop, which will never happen if he is allowed to treat the whole thing as a huge joke.

The first essential, therefore, is discipline; but don't overdo it or the dog may become so obedient that he lies down on command and stays in the doorway while someone drags you into the garden! It is unlikely, however, that that will be your problem. The question is much more likely to be: who controls the position, you or the dog? If you have a strong-headed dog you can strengthen what control you have on the down by adding the control you have on the lead. Put the dog on the lead when someone comes to the door and, if he attempts to rush out, in either an aggressive or an over-friendly manner, you can correct him with a very firm 'No' and a sharp jerk as described in heel work. Then *make* him lie down and allow you to bring the visitor in, when he can be praised by you.

The aggressive dog should be handled and spoken to by the visitor (provided he or she knows how to handle a dog) to impress on it that all strangers are not enemies. The less petting an over-friendly dog gets from strangers the better. Some people maintain that to be any good as a guard a dog must never be petted by strangers, but I have never found that to be the case. No dog should be encouraged to welcome every Tom, Dick or Harry and dogs with a tendency to do so should be checked from the start. (I only wish some means could be found to check Tom, Dick and Harry, their wives and families, from interfering with dogs belonging to other people!) If the dog will either come when called or go down *quickly* on command, that should present no difficulty and is a better method than the often recommended one of getting as many people as possible to wallop the dog when he makes friends with them. In theory, that should be a good idea, but in practice the first snag is finding the people and the second is that all dogs, even friendly ones, do not care to be clouted by a complete stranger. The result is that they develop a strong dislike for strangers, and who can blame them?

If a dog is not over-friendly, and more especially if he shows signs of being suspicious of strangers, I think it is a good idea to get as many different, and understanding, people as possible to make friends with him. You are trying to let the dog know that if you are with him and say it is O.K., it *is* O.K. Most sensible dogs will realize that, but many that would be sensible are made aggressive by owners who, by clutching at them if a stranger approaches, arouse the instinct of danger.

And now something about dogs which bark at a stranger, or a strange sound, and won't stop. Unless nipped in the bud this will soon become a most objectionable habit. If the dog barks when on a lead it is easy to check him, as correction can be applied *as* the dog barks. Put him on the lead, let him bark at someone at the door as usual, then give the command 'Quiet' followed by a sharp jerk as the next bark is on its way. This jerk, at the right time, will literally stop the bark and the dog should immediately be praised. If it starts again say 'Quiet', and if it does not stop at once repeat with a harder jerk each time until it does.

I once travelled with a lady who had a dog that kept up the most irritating little bark throughout the journey. Every time he barked the owner stroked him and, in a most encouraging tone, said, 'Now be a good boy, just be quiet,' whereupon the dog would immediately bark again. This went on for about three hours! But it was not a noisy dog. Had the owner given it a sharp jerk with a severe 'No' or 'Quiet' *as it barked*, followed by praise *as it remained quiet* I am certain it would have caused no further trouble.

If difficulty is experienced in getting a dog to respond to 'Quiet', it is sometimes worth teaching him to 'Speak' and cease speaking on command. It is easy to teach a noisy dog to speak by getting him excited or showing him food and, like the lady mentioned above, rewarding him the moment he barks. Once you have got him to bark on command, teach him to stop as described above, the advantage being that you can practise this until the dog really understands the command and will start *and* stop barking immediately on command, even if some distance away.

You may feel that if you go to the door to greet a visitor

it would be rather rude to start training your dog. With that I agree, but the initial disciplinary exercises already described should have been taught in some quiet spot. To put them into practice you can enlist the help of a friend or member of the family. If someone suddenly bangs on the door, a keen guard or a noisy dog will not stop to think that it is someone he knows. Go to the door with the dog, put him down and open the door. When he sees a friend he will want to make a fuss, and that is when you can test your control. If you say 'Down' it means down, no matter what the dog thinks or who is there. If this is practised sufficiently, many dogs will take up their position without any command as such, but simply because you go to open the door, which is another of those good habits. You open the door and there is the dog, no danger to a friend but a strong deterrent to an enemy.

To me it seems tragic that many dogs are destroyed as dangerous whose one and only motive was to protect their master or mistress. An over-developed guarding instinct can, of course, render a dog very dangerous indeed, but many which bite people would never have done so had they been properly trained. If you want a dog that will protect you, if necessary, you *must* be able and willing to train it to absolute obedience. Only two things are needed: that he will come to you when called; that he will lie down at your feet and stay there. Even if he won't come back, so long as you can drop him before he reaches the 'victim' there is no danger. In any case, the best guards do not usually rush at people in the distance. If there is danger, the first thing a good natural guard will do is rush to the person or object it is guarding; if it does not do that instinctively, it should be taught to do so right from the start.

None of the advice given above applies to the *so-called* good 'house dog' which rushes around barking hysterically but never goes nearer to a stranger than to nip him in the back of the leg, then disappear. The only advice I can give concerning such a dog is to get rid of it and try again.

Perhaps the most prevalent cause of dogs biting their owners arises from the guarding instinct. Apart from dogs with bad temperaments, there are far too many which bite, or threaten to bite, their owners and get into the habit of doing it. More often than not this starts in quite a young puppy which decides to guard its bone. 'Of course,' says the stupid owner, 'that's only natural,' and calls the family, who stand around and laugh. To show just 'what a little devil he is' one of them pretends he is going to take the bone, whereupon the puppy bares his teeth and growls.

All very funny, very funny indeed, but anyone who does that sort of thing deserves to get bitten, as they very often do. Of course it is natural for a puppy to guard a bone, but no more natural than to chase sheep, and it should not be allowed to do either. What really happens when a puppy snaps or bares his teeth and you draw back? In no time you have crashed off your pedestal as the master and are down to the level of an eight-weeks-old puppy. Gone in a flash is any respect he may have had for you. He is now the boss. Depending on the puppy, this state of affairs quickly or slowly goes from bad to worse— never gets better—but just how much worse it *can* get is fantastic. If the dog takes a fancy to anything he just says, as he did with the bone, 'You can't have it'—and you *don't* have it.

Oh, I am not exaggerating. Some people brought a seven-months-old puppy to me one day which, on the previous day, had taken possession of the front door mat, refusing to allow the wife to go out or the husband to come in! Even more amusing was the case of a young bridegroom-to-be who bought a Miniature Poodle puppy as a wedding present for his fiancée. As the puppy grew up, he gradually took possession of anything he fancied, resenting most strongly being disturbed when he had settled down for a nap. He slept on the bed and never appeared to have any objection to his owners going to bed. What he did object to was their moving in bed and, if they did, he bit them through the bedclothes! Both husband and wife were permanently bruised!

You would be amazed at the number of able-bodied men who, quite unashamedly, will say that their three-months-old puppy won't let them pick up his bone or won't let them move him off the hearth. A three-months-old puppy, a canine child, *won't let them*! In such cases I usually ask, 'If I were to slap your face or threaten to punch your nose for no reason at all, what would you do?' Strangely enough the reply is almost invariably, 'I'd hit you back.' When I ask why they don't do that to the puppy I am usually told: 'Oh, I never hit him. I thought that might make him worse. I never thought a dog would turn nasty with anyone who was always kind to it.' That depends on the dog and on what is meant by kindness. Such a dog is rarely nasty, it is merely cheeky and disrespectful, and is following its natural instinct to protect its own property. Very often it does it through sheer devilment, for the fun of seeing how afraid its stupid owner can be! Often it ends up by being sentenced to death as a savage dog, entirely owing to an owner having been too 'kind', or too frightened, to retaliate *on the very first symptoms* of this habit developing.

Let us suppose that you have a puppy or a young dog lying in front of the fire; you go to push him over and he bares his teeth or snaps at your hand. You may be afraid; if it is the first time he has done it you will probably be surprised. You draw your hand back quickly and leave him alone. 'Fine,' says the pup, 'that's just what I wanted,' and settles down to sleep.

Suppose, however, the hand at which he snapped hits him right across the face? Instead of you being afraid of the puppy he is afraid of you, and will no doubt remove himself from the hearth in double-quick time. Unkind, you may think, but certainly not so unkind as letting a dog become boss. This is not merely a question of refusing to move from the hearth; it is a question of principle, affecting the whole relationship between you and your dog. Many dogs will 'speak back' to their owners but *under no circumstances* should they be allowed to get away with it. This is not a case of developing an instinct and keeping it under control, it is a case of stamping it out *for good*.

Points to bear in mind are: (1) Don't hesitate; a quick rap is more effective than a hard one, and remember what I said earlier about the dog reacting to the trainer's fear. (2) Don't shout; don't say anything at all, for that will warn the puppy and reduce the shock. (3) Don't prepare to punish the puppy by searching for something to hit him with; hit him with your hand and, even if he does bite, there are far worse fates than that. (4) Never threaten by showing a whip or promising what you will do if he does not behave; *do it*, or leave him alone.

Remember to praise the puppy. Even if he did not really

want to do so, if he moves from the hearth he has obeyed, and you must reward him. If you frighten him and he runs to the other side of the room, this reward is of the utmost importance. Call him in a very friendly tone and make a great fuss of him. You may think that is being inconsistent—scolding one minute and petting the next—but you are actually scolding him for being naughty and praising him for being good (coming to you). In this way he will soon learn that life is very pleasant *so long as he is good*. He will not lose his confidence in you and, most important of all, he will grow to *respect* you. As in all training, *don't nag*.

You may think that what I have just said about rapping a puppy on the face contradicts what I previously said about making a dog afraid of the hand he should trust. Up to a point that is true, as the object is that, instead of him frightening you, you frighten him. You must therefore *immediately* make a point of winning back any confidence you may have lost. Provided it has a good temperament the puppy that does this sort of thing is not usually easily put off. The reason for using the hand is because it is speed that counts.

Although the same in principle, puppies that guard a bone have to be treated rather differently. If you give such a puppy a rap on the face he will run away, more than likely taking his bone with him. The best way is to treat him in exactly the same way as the puppy chewing the rug. If you put your hand towards his bone the puppy will probably bite, but if you put your hand towards the puppy himself he is unlikely to do so. Having got him firmly by the scruff he *cannot* bite you and you can get him to release the bone by shaking and tapping on the nose. *Immediately* he releases the bone praise the puppy and give him the bone back, in order to let him understand that you are not trying to steal his bone but only showing him that what you say goes, without question. Remember that if light correction has no effect you must increase the dose until it does.

As I have already said, if this action is taken the very first time a puppy shows signs of disrespect further trouble is unlikely. Occasionally, however, one meets a really aggressive type on which ordinary corrective methods only have the effect of making him more determined to win. Such dogs, especially big ones, are dangerous and, although sometimes exceptional workers, I fail to see how anyone can derive pleasure from owning one as a companion.

Jealousy

One of the characteristics arising from the guarding instinct is jealousy. It appears to take the same form in the dog as it does in the human. As there are few humans who have never at any time felt a little bit jealous, there should be few dog owners who cannot understand a jealous dog. In many cases all that is necessary to see *why* a dog is jealous is to put yourself in his shoes. Having found out the cause of the trouble it is sometimes a simple matter to remove it.

A jealous dog will want to attack a rival, but usually only when the rival appears to be attracting too much of the owner's attention. If the dog respects the owner and knows better than to attack, it is likely that he will go into a 'big huff' and sulk. A dog cannot help being jealous any more than a person can. Training will help the owner to keep a jealous dog under control, but it will not remove the jealousy. Trying to 'knock it out of him' will usually make matters worse.

Quite a number of dogs are jealous of a new baby in the household. They are usually made worse by the fact that parents, quite naturally and perhaps unconsciously, protect the child from the dog. My advice is to get rid of the dog. If your dog is jealous of your boy-friend you can hope that it will get over it. You may even get a new boy-friend that your dog likes! To take such risks with a baby is, I think, very foolish. It is also unkind to the dog to force it to live in a constant state of jealousy with this (to it) awful yelling creature receiving all the attention it so much wants to have. A dog cannot help being jealous, but in different circumstances (in a new home, for instance) it may be no trouble.

Fighting

Jealousy is often the cause of dogs fighting but, as I said in Part I, fighters can be divided roughly into three groups. How to deal with them can be divided, again roughly, in the same way.

(1) *Dogs that fight for the sake of fighting, and thoroughly enjoy it.* These are usually good dogs with firm, bold temperaments;

often very hard dogs. To have any success with such a dog you will have to be firm, even hard, in your training. You must make him realize that the slightest attempt to fight has most unpleasant results. It is no good waiting until he *is* fighting, as a fighting dog, like a man who has completely lost his temper, is oblivious to everything except the fight. Remember, too, that, even when he is only attempting to fight, he is 'seeing red'. To talk to him then, or to correct him in the usual way, will have no effect at all. If you really set about a young dog of this type on his first two or three attempts to fight, he may develop a healthy respect for you. He will then be much more likely to leave other dogs when you tell him, even if his desire to fight is just as strong.

(2) *Dogs that fight because of the guarding instinct, and which will only attack another dog if it approaches their master or comes on to their property.* Often these dogs are devils on a lead but perfectly safe running loose amongst other dogs. The point to note is that they can't help it. The guarding instinct (or jealousy) *compels* them to attack and any attempt to 'knock it out of him' may create a complex, making matters worse. By obedience training, however, you should be able to get the dog absolutely under control, enabling you to avoid circumstances likely to lead to a fight. If, by accident, a dog should become involved, he must be severely corrected to avoid the impression that you agree with him.

(3) *Dogs that fight through fear*—are best avoided altogether! You will have noticed that I have used the words 'may' and 'should' a lot. Although I have had quite a number of fighters to cope with, including some *real* fighters that were quite exceptional dogs in every other way, the answer to the problem is difficult to find. There are, however, many dogs which have become fighters owing entirely to the mistakes made by their owners. It might, therefore, be worth mentioning some of those mistakes.

Let us imagine Mrs. X out for a walk with Towser. She sees another dog approaching (Towser hasn't seen it), so she yells in an almost hysterical tone at Towser to 'Come here'. If Towser understands 'Come here', its meaning is completely obliterated by the terror-stricken tone of voice. Instinctively he wants to protect his mistress from whatever is frightening her and, looking around, finds that a dog is just appearing. Quite naturally, he attacks it. Many dogs that have little natural inclination to do so are taught to fight in that way.

Mrs. X would have done better to have given Towser some simple obedience training. When she saw the other dog she could then have called him to heel and passed by without further trouble.

Often I see ladies carrying a stick or umbrella to 'shoo off' strange dogs. When I was a boy, my father bought a hunt terrier pup to kill rats. As it showed no inclination to do so by the time it was six months old, and having no patience to wait until the instinct developed, he put it in an empty water-tank with one. This was a big, fierce rat which attacked the poor pup, terrifying him until he cried to be lifted out. Had I protested I should have been told not to be so soft, but, eventually, the pup was lifted out and the rat killed. One day soon after, while this 'useless creature' was awaiting its fate, he was following my father round a stack when a rat popped out. My father made a swipe at it, and missed—but the pup had it like a flash, killing it instantly. From that day on—from that second, in fact—that dog would tackle anything that lived.

In that case, of course, it was the instinct to kill which was aroused in a dog bred for nothing else. My reason for mentioning it is because it was aroused by the dog's natural desire to join in anything its master does. If you threaten another dog, your dog will (if he's a real dog) want to help you. That is a sure way of encouraging him to fight and you have no idea how keen he will become until he starts.

Another point worth remembering is that a dog which continually meets different dogs from puppyhood is much less inclined to fight than those which do not. The risk, of course, is that one day he may meet one which starts a scrap. Once a dog starts fighting, I have been unable to find any cure, although it should be possible to keep him under control by training.

In this country, overrun with dogs which appear either to have no owners or owners who, even when present, just couldn't care less, a dog that wants to fight can be an awful problem. It is, therefore, worth taking great care to find one with little inclination to do so.

CHASING

Understanding of what I have already said in the chapters concerning the hunting and pack instincts is likely to be more helpful than what I have to tell you now about chasing. I should also like to repeat that this habit, which arises from the development of the hunting instinct, can, in many cases, be prevented, but can never be cured in the true sense of the word. Fortunately, it is usually possible to keep it under control by training. The prevalent idea that shooting is the only cure for a dog that has once chased sheep shows how great is the lack of dog sense in this country.

So far as chasing livestock is concerned, the biggest snag for you, the average dog owner, is that you have no animals of your own on which to train your puppy. We keep a variety of livestock and if I get a young dog that has not been brought up with other animals, the first thing I expect to have to do is teach him not to chase them. While admitting that having other animals is a help in teaching dogs not to chase, I think the chief causes of this chasing problem are lack of dog sense and missing the opportunities which *do* occur. There is a wide variety of 'quarry' for dogs to chase, some better subjects on which to train a dog than others. The best are probably the wild rabbit and the domestic cat, and few dog owners do not come across both from time to time.

In the case of the cat, the chase almost invariably ends with the dog baying its 'quarry' up a tree, down a drain or in some other place of safety, and that is the golden opportunity which the average owner always throws away. Instead of yelling in the distance, go straight up to him, when the chances are he will either not see you coming or, if he does, will ignore you, thus making it easy for you to get hold of him and give him the worst hiding he has ever had. This is not correction now; it is punishment, which you hope is going to prevent the development of a really bad habit. If he is not too big, shake him as already described until you feel he must be giddy; if he is too big for that, give him a good punch in the ribs. And, if you feel you are being cruel, remember that you are not being half so cruel to your dog as he would like to be to the unfortunate cat!

If you do that the *first* time your dog chases a cat you may never have to do it again, and if you repeat it *every* time he does it you *should* be able to stop him. In most cases when this *cannot* be done the hunting instinct is so strong that it makes the dog unsuitable as a pet.

As a practical example of this, we might take a Labrador I once trained. This dog had been allowed to 'chase fur' since a puppy, which meant that, whenever the door was open, he was off rabbiting for hours, sometimes days. Apart from rendering him useless as a gundog, the purpose for which he was bought, this habit made his farmer owners most unpopular with their neighbours. After sending him to a well-known gun-dog trainer who advised shooting him, they came to me as a last resort.

One day, not long after I had him, he got off my ground on to three or four hundred acres of adjoining country which abounded with hares. Of course, he could not catch a hare, but as one disappeared in the distance another would pop up in front of him, and away he went again—me panting along some way behind, hoping, rather optimistically, that an obliging hare would come my way, enabling me to catch the dog as he followed it.

By the time he had chased seven or eight hares he was exhausted and packed it up. But when I called him, would he come to me? No fear; he had had far too many hidings for that. Instead he slunk off and hid behind a haystack about half a mile away. I followed till I could see him crouching beside the stack, but I did not do what most people would have done, and several people had already done—most un-successfully—go up to him and give him a good hiding. I halted a little way off, stooped down and called him to me in a very persuasive, friendly tone. He was a bit suspicious, but crept slowly towards me and, when he did come up, I made a great fuss of him. I then put him on a lead in case, now he had got his wind back, he saw another hare; and we had a nice friendly walk home.

He did that several times, but, after this, would always come straight back to me when he had had enough. I had not stopped him chasing hares, but I had got him to come back. A dog that runs away and comes back is always to be preferred to one that runs away and won't come back.

In training dogs I find that opportunities usually come to

those who wait. The trouble is they are often gone before one has time to realize it. Anyhow, my opportunity did come and I seized it with both hands. It was one morning before break-fast that he put up a rabbit in a clump of long grass; a most co-operative rabbit, which refused to bolt out of this cover. The dog kept dashing round in zig-zags after the rabbit, and I kept dashing round in zig-zags after the dog, and, by good luck rather than any athletic prowess, I won! As you may have gathered, this was a hard, wilful dog, but, by the time I had finished with him, he had no doubts whatsoever as to whether chasing rabbits was a pleasant or unpleasant pastime!

That one lesson did not entirely remove his interest in fur. It was, however, the turning-point at which he started to be an asset instead of the liability he had previously been. He had lots of intelligence and in less than six weeks I handled him in a working gundog test, where, although he did not win any-thing, he was well under control. Had the owners checked that dog the *first* time he chased a rabbit, probably as a puppy when he could have been much more easily caught, it is almost certain that he would have given no further trouble. It would also have saved him the very severe punishment that he had from me as an alternative to being destroyed.

'But,' I can almost hear you say, 'I don't mind if my dog does chase rabbits, it's motor-cars and sheep I want to stop him chasing.' The basic principles of training to stop dogs chasing any kind of quarry are the same. When I got Quiz, the Alsatian to whom I have already referred, she had a mania for rabbiting. Even when she could neither see nor smell any, she was always wondering where there might be rabbits. Before she was of any use to me, therefore, I had to break this mania, which I did, partly by very severe and continued correction and partly by diverting her energy and instincts into other channels. I taught her to chase a man she could catch instead of rabbits which almost invariably got away; to hunt for objects she could find and bring back to me instead of running wild all over the countryside.

The interesting point is that I had no trouble at all in teaching her to leave the 'criminal' running away, generally regarded as one of the most difficult exercises in police dog training. This was simply because I had taught her, not only to leave rabbits, but to come when I called her—no matter what the distraction.

Incidentally, this bitch, who showed little affection for anyone when I first had her, became quite devoted to me. She lost all interest in going off on her own and eventually was reluctant to go anywhere without me, even when the other dogs were taken out for a walk.

For the novice, I think by far the best method to stop a dog chasing is the check cord. It is also the safest, as there is less danger of building up a wrong association of ideas and of any harm to the 'quarry'. So long as you do not go too near them, you can actually take a dog that is liable to chase among livestock.

Put the dog on the check cord, holding him quite short, and when a car, a bike, a sheep or whatever it is that the dog chases appears—or rather as it disappears—let the dog go as in the lower picture in Plate IX. When he almost reaches the end of the cord shout 'Down' or call his name in a harsh tone and the check cord will do the rest. If you have ordered him to 'Down', repeat the command as soon as he has got over his somersault, see that he goes down where he is, go to him and praise him. If you have called him back, see that he does so, with the aid of the cord if necessary, and again praise him.

The faster the dog is going at the time of the 'check' the more effective will the lesson be, and it is up to you to see that he associates it with the word of command. Some people are under the impression that this treatment will break a dog's neck. It is, in fact, a very old method, used extensively amongst gundog trainers to stop over-keen dogs 'running in', and I have never heard of a dog injuring itself in any way.

Unless you are able to coil a rope so that you can play it out without getting it tangled, it is best to let it drag on the ground behind you in a large loop (Plate IX [b] again). It is of the utmost importance, too, to vary the length, otherwise the dog may very soon learn to measure his distance and be able to judge almost to an inch when he is out of range. Check him sometimes when he is quite close to you by putting your foot on the cord as it runs past you on the ground, and at others let him run right to the end before checking him.

If you have a dog that is really keen on chasing a stick or a ball (whether he retrieves it properly does not matter), you can, by the use of the check cord, teach him not to chase, in your own garden. If he is not very keen you may put him off playing this game altogether, but if he is keen you should be able to send him after the ball and, *while it is still running away*, either drop him or call him back. That will be no guarantee that you will be able to do the same thing if he sees sheep, but it will be a great help. The only reason why it may not is that to some dogs sheep are much more exciting quarry. What is quite certain is that if you cannot stop him on a dead object you will not stop him if he wants to chase something alive.

There is a rather prevalent idea that to cure a dog of chasing any class of livestock, all that is necessary is to allow it to be attacked by a particularly aggressive member of the particular species. As I have already said, man has bred dogs to attack animals much bigger and more ferocious than themselves. If the above theory worked in practice a terrier which got bitten by a rat would never chase another, and a cattle dog that got kicked by a bullock would keep away from cattle. With real dogs such experiences usually make them all the keener—if perhaps a little more careful! There is, in fact, no more reason why a ferocius ram should teach a dog not to chase sheep than that the dog should teach the sheep not to chase dogs. Being a beast of prey, a real dog, even a little one, with plenty of 'guts', combined with active mind and body, is more than a match for any sheep.

We have a herd of goats, all of which are reared more or less amongst the dogs, usually on the best of terms. Occasionally, however, one becomes belligerent, thinking it great fun to butt the dogs. According to some people, that should put them off chasing goats. In fact, it merely annoys them, although they remain quite friendly towards the other goats. They will even gang up as a pack and, unless we are careful, will sort out this creature which has challenged their superiority, with the obvious intention of 'fixing it'. Quite apart from the fate of the goat, to allow the dogs to have it out, far from teaching them not to chase goats, would merely encourage them to attack all goats.

There *are* dogs which can be intimidated into giving other

animals a wide berth. These are (1) dogs which would also run away if their owner were attacked and (2) puppies still too young to have confidence in themselves. For the former I have little use and if I could find no more humane method of teaching puppies not to chase I should give up training.

Perhaps I should mention here that a puppy, brought up from an early age with another animal, will often accept it as a friend, like Sloopy and Creamy in Plate II [c]. A dog will sometimes protect its own cat from other dogs or even from humans; but it does not follow that it will treat all cats in the same way. Dogs recognize strangers on four legs just as easily as they do those on two. As an example of this, we changed our stud goat, taking the old one away and bringing the other back at night. Both were white and, being at the end of the breeding season, the one smelt just as badly as the other to me! When the dogs were let out in the morning they were furious to find a stranger in the male goat paddock.

Just as amusing was an old Border Collie bitch I had who used to spend her time getting the hens up into a bunch and keeping them there. At that time I had a neighbour whose rooster made a habit of visiting my hens. If he happened to be there when Tot was let out she would, instead of gathering them all into a bunch, sort out this intruder and march him straight home, never halting until he was back in his own garden. This was due, not to any idea of acting as chaperon, but simply to the instinct to keep strangers off her own ground.

PLATE XIII

The right (*left*) and wrong positions for a dog to be most effective as a guard

PLATE XIV

Retrieving a tennis ball can be used to practise control and at the
same time to provide exercise for the dog
(*Sally Anne Thompson*)

CHAPTER X

PRACTICAL EXERCISES

Retrieving and Allied Exercises

HAVING made several references to the importance of giving a dog something to do, I feel I ought to include some advice on the sort of things you may be able to teach your dog. Being the versatile animals they are, it is impossible to select any exercise and say that is the one for your dog, especially when we remember that it may be impossible to teach one dog something another will do without any training. Also, what may be a useful exercise to one owner may be useless to another.

One of the most useful exercises to any dog owner, and one from which the majority of dogs derive great pleasure, is the retrieve, either in its simple form or in one of its variations. There are two generally accepted methods of teaching the retrieve: one through play and the other by what is known as the German or forcing method. My experience is that the best and quickest results are obtained by combining the two, the extent to which each is used depending on the dog being trained and, in some degree, on the skill of the trainer. As they are so different I shall have to explain them separately, and leave it to you to decide how best to apply either, or both, to the training of your dog.

To teach a dog to retrieve in play is, strictly speaking, not training; it is merely encouraging an instinct to develop, and the ease with which this can be done depends mainly on its strength in the first place. That the instinct is present in most dogs is proved by the many thousands of people who succeed in teaching their dogs to carry various objects.

In teaching by this method you are entirely dependent on reward—correction must be left right out. You therefore cannot *make* a dog retrieve in this way. The instinct to retrieve, however, will make the dog pick up and carry an object provided it is originally strong enough and is encouraged in the right way. All you have to do is to get the dog to bring the object to you instead of careering round the garden with it as one so often sees. Dogs taught in this way are often just as reliable as those taught by the forcing method.

With all instincts the time either to encourage or suppress is when they show signs of developing on their own. Any setback at that stage may be difficult to get over later. If, therefore, your puppy brings to you in triumph your best hat, don't scold him. Take it from him gently (it will do the hat less harm anyhow), praise him, and put it well out of his reach. If he starts to rip it to pieces, that is a different matter and should be checked.

To encourage a puppy to retrieve, you can make use of the instinct to hunt, from which the retrieve is derived. Start when he is in a playful mood, throw an object (not a stone) along the ground so that it 'runs' away from him. It is almost certain that he will chase this 'prey' and the chances are he will pick it up, especially if he reaches it before it has stopped moving. As he reaches the object, when his mind is on it, tell him to 'Carry' or 'Fetch', in a very enthusiastic tone, to try and get him to associate this command (really a request in this case) with picking up an object. If he does pick it up, repeat 'Carry, carry' in the same encouraging tone. As you do, either squat down and call him to you exactly as you have been in the habit of doing, or run away from him calling him to follow. If he brings the object to you, praise him lavishly and take it from him gently.

He may want to keep it, and it is of the utmost importance not to hurt him in getting it out of his mouth. Place the left hand across his muzzle so that you can press on his lips with the fingers on one side and the thumb on the other, hold the object in the right hand (don't pull it) and, to a firm command such as 'Drop it', gently press the lips against the gums (*see* Plate VIII [*b*]). Increase the pressure *gradually* until he releases his hold; remove the object with the right hand and immediately release the pressure with the left; change the tone of voice and praise lavishly.

The easiest way to make a puppy release its hold on an object is to offer a piece of meat in exchange, and this is, in most cases, a good idea. The only risk is that, with a greedy

puppy, the thought of food may take his mind right off retrieving. As a result he may drop the object before reaching
you—or he may not even go after it to start with!

Suppose, now, that you throw something and the puppy
chases it (if he won't you might as well give up the idea of
teaching the retrieve in play) but when he reaches it he refuses
to pick it up. Don't keep on telling him to 'Carry', as he has
no idea what that command means and you will merely be
getting him accustomed to a sound that means nothing. Walk
up to the object, kick it or throw it along the ground, and try
again, but don't go on trying too long. One day you may find
that he will pick up the object. The aim in retrieving, however,
is not only to pick up an object but also to bring it straight
back and 'deliver tenderly to hand', as it is termed in gundog
circles. There is little use in having a dog which will carry an
egg if, on returning to you, he spits it out at your feet. There is
even less use in one that picks up an object and dashes off in
the opposite direction!

These and other bad habits, such as dashing after the
object before you have given the command, can be avoided,
or kept under control, by simple obedience and by resorting
to some of the methods used in teaching the retrieve by force.
As you know, the disciplinary exercises I have described are
all based on correction as much as reward, and the important
point in applying them now is to avoid any risk of a wrong
association of ideas being built up. For instance, if a puppy
picks up an object and dashes off with it, you might be tempted
to throw something after him as I described in teaching a
puppy to come when called. The risk in doing so, however, is
far too great, for, while the puppy might associate this correction with running away, it might just as easily associate it with
picking up an object, and you may succeed in 'curing' it for
life of picking up anything. Actually, the usual mistake is that
the owner runs towards the puppy instead of running away
from it, so that, instead of a game where the puppy fetches
something for its master, we have a sort of hide and seek with
the puppy always winning. For young dogs which are really
keen on carrying objects but refuse to retrieve properly, the
check cord is probably the best means of getting them under
control.

The first essential in teaching the retrieve in play is to wait until the puppy is really keen on retrieving before you attempt to control him in any way. Some puppies are bred to retrieve and *must* be controlled when quite young to prevent their carrying anything and everything all over the place. Others are much less keen, and the instinct, which can usually be encouraged, can be just as easily discouraged in the early stages by trying to make the puppy retrieve *properly* instead of just encouraging him to retrieve.

If you have followed the foregoing advice and find that your dog still refuses to retrieve, you can still use the forcing method, and I have yet to find a dog I could not teach in this way. Some people, however, experience great difficulty in teaching the retrieve this way and it requires much more skill and patience. It is sometimes maintained, particularly by gun-dog trainers, that a dog trained by this method is never so keen on retrieving as one that does so naturally. With that I disagree. I have found that once a dog knows that it *must* do it, and that it pleases its master by retrieving, the instinct itself appears to develop. By then turning it into a game, I have found that most dogs taught by this method become just as keen as those which retrieve naturally.

It has, in fact, two advantages over the previous one. Firstly, by teaching the dog that it *must* pick up something on command you can make him pick up *any* object at *any* time. Secondly, by going forward carefully one step at a time you can, if you come up against some unexpected obstacle, go back one step at a time until you come to the step where you find it possible to start again. If, in teaching by the method already mentioned, something puts the dog off, you are sunk, as you depend entirely on the instinct to retrieve, which may not be strong enough to overcome the obstacle. The only thing to do then is to go right back to the beginning and start the method I am about to describe.

In teaching by this method, which is really a modification of the methods used on the Continent, a wooden dumb-bell is used almost universally. This is easy for a dog to pick up, which in turn makes it easier for the trainer to *make* the dog pick it up. The dumb-bell should be light and its ends should be comfortably clear of the lips.

Do not start trying to teach the retrieve by this method until you have succeeded in instilling some sort of obedience into your dog. He must sit still and pay attention to what you are trying to explain to him, otherwise you will be trying to teach him two things at the same time.

Make your dog sit in the usual position by your left side, with lead on. Holding the dumb-bell in your right hand, put your left hand over his face and press the lips against the gums gently as in teaching a puppy to let go. This will force him to open his mouth. As he does so, give the command 'Carry' and, with the right hand, place the dumb-bell in the dog's mouth. He will almost certainly try to spit it out. It is up to you to see that he does not; it is essential that he realizes, before you finish this exercise, that he MUST hold the dumb-bell. Some dogs offer no resistance but with others you will have to be firm, at the same time being careful not to hurt the lips or gums, which would make him even more resentful. Keep giving the command 'Carry' in a firm tone and hold his jaws shut on the dumb-bell until he stops struggling. Immediately he does so, change your tone of voice completely and instantly praise him, and remove the dumb-bell from his mouth with the command 'Drop it'.

He may have given up struggling only for a breather, and if you try to make him hold the dumb-bell for any length of time the chances are that he will start struggling again. If you can get him to hold it for a second and take it when *you* want him to, you will have gone one step forward. But if you get him to hold it for a minute, and he then succeeds in spitting it out when *he* wants to, you will have gone several steps backwards. Continue on these lines, making the time the dog holds the dumb-bell gradually longer, until he will allow you to put the dumb-bell in his mouth and will hold it for quite an appreciable time without resentment.

Having got the dog to allow you to put the dumb-bell in his mouth, and hold it, the next stage is to get him to take it himself. Do not go on opening his mouth and shoving the dumb-bell into it indefinitely. Hold the dumb-bell just touching his lips and, with the fingers and thumb of the left hand in the same position as before, give the command 'Carry'. You may have to press the lips very gently, but if you do it properly

the dog should soon open his mouth on command in anticipation of the pressure on the lips. Often the first indication that he
is about to respond is that he licks the dumb-bell or opens his
mouth very slightly, though not sufficiently to take the dumb-
bell. If he does, encourage him in a praising tone of voice and
he will probably open his mouth and take it. You must immediately praise him very generously. It is a good idea to finish
the lesson at that point.

Up to now the dumb-bell has been going to the dog. The
next stage is to get the dog to go to the dumb-bell and grasp
it himself. This is done by continuing as in the preceding
paragraph, gradually holding the dumb-bell farther and
farther away from the dog. At first he can stretch his neck to
reach it, but soon he will have to get up from his sitting
position and move forward, which he should be encouraged
to do. If he refuses to go forward you will have to make him
move by jerking the collar, gently at first, then more severely
if necessary. With a sensitive dog that resents this, it is sometimes better to push him forward with the hand on the back
of the neck. Continue from there until you can hold the dumb-
bell in front of you and the dog will, on command, get up from
a sitting position beside you, go forward and take it. When he
does, you can move back a step and he will bring it to you, so
that you have now got the dog going forward for an article
and bringing it back to you—the basis of retrieving.

The next stage is often a difficult one—getting the dog to
pick up the dumb-bell off the ground. Many dogs will take an
article quite cheerfully from the handler's hand, even when he
holds it on the ground, but take the hand away and they won't
touch it. You can encourage the dog to pick up by putting the
dumb-bell on the ground and, as you give the command
'Carry', make it 'live' by moving it slightly with the right hand.
If this does not work you may have to use quite a lot of force.
By now your dog understands the command and, if he cannot
be persuaded to pick up the dumb-bell, you must push his
head down to it and *make* him.

Having got the dog to go forward a few steps, pick up the
dumb-bell and bring it to you, all you have to do next is to
put the dumb-bell farther and farther away until the dog will
go right out to the end of the lead, pick it up and bring it back.

To make the distance a little greater you can advance a step
as he goes forward and take a step back as he comes towards
you. When you can rely on the dog doing this—and not before
—you can remove the lead, throw the dumb-bell about the
same distance as before, give the command and the dog should
go forward, pick it up and bring it back. He will, in fact,
retrieve, and you can go on gradually increasing the distance
until he will go as far as you can throw the dumb-bell.

If you aspire to working your dog in obedience competitions you will have to teach him to bring the dumb-bell right
up to you, sit in front and hold it until the judge tells you to
take it from him. In gundog circles, however (and, after all,
the main function of a gundog is to retrieve), that is regarded
as a waste of time; all that is asked is that a dog shall put the
object in the hand of the handler without the latter having to
stoop down. The chief points are that the dog will bring the
object straight back *quickly* (there is little sense in teaching a
dog to do something you can do more quickly yourself), and
that it will not play with the object or mouth it, thereby
probably damaging it. To achieve that it is a good idea,
irrespective of the method used, to teach the dog to come right
up to you and hold the object until you decide to take it, not
until *he* decides to give it to you.

Here the common mistake is to go forward and take the
dumb-bell. Never go towards your dog; always make the dog
come to you. If he sits too far away, move backwards and keep
coaxing him up until you get him exactly where you want him,
sitting squarely with his head right up to you. Then praise him
well and take the dumb-bell. It may be necessary to put him
on a lead to get him right up to you, which is essential for
competition work.

It is very important to praise well at the right psychological
moment. For example, you throw the dumb-bell, giving the
command 'Carry' firmly; your dog walks to it, not very
willingly, looks at it and then looks at you as if to say 'Must
I?' You then give an even firmer 'Carry' and he opens his
mouth to pick it up. If, at that moment, you say 'Carry, carry'
in a very enthusiastic and encouraging tone, at the same time
running backwards and patting your hands against your thighs,
the chances are that he will pick up the dumb-bell and rush

up to you with it. If you just stand and look stupid he will probably either mouth the dumb-bell and come back without it or pick it up and return at a slow walk, head and tail down, which is not what is wanted.

If your dog is steady on the sit whilst you throw the dumb-bell, will hold it for a reasonable time and deliver properly to hand, you can speed up his retrieve by playing with him, and I always finish a retrieving lesson in that way. Having got a dog to do a 'serious' retrieve I make a fuss of him, get him excited and, without bothering about sitting, throw the dumb-bell as far as I can, preferably into long grass or other cover, and let him rush off to find it. When he does I run in the opposite direction so that he will come galloping after me, and I take it from him without worrying about finish. Never keep on until the dog has had enough; always finish a lesson when he is still asking for more.

Quite often a playful dog will mouth the dumb-bell when he brings it back. If he does, tap him under the chin with your hand, at the same time scolding him, and do not take the dumb-bell from him until he holds it properly. When he stops mouthing it praise him, give the command 'Drop it' and take the dumb-bell. Gradually increase the time he holds it until you have a dog that will sit and hold a dumb-bell until you are ready to take it.

In anticipation of 'Drop it' many dogs are inclined to drop the dumb-bell as the handler puts his hand down to take it. This can be prevented by putting your hand under the dog's chin, as though you intended taking the dumb-bell, but give the command 'Carry' and make him hold it until you say 'Drop it'.

So much for teaching a dog to pick up a visible object and bring it back to you, no doubt great fun for the dog and maybe quite a help in exercising him. To the owner, however, it is of little practical value, as he could just as easily pick up the object himself.

A dog that will retrieve and has initiative can easily be taught to find hidden objects with the aid of its nose; which, of course, no human being could do. Start by throwing the object into long grass so that the dog sees it fall but has to use his nose to find it. Give him the usual command to carry and it is likely that he will hunt until he finds the article and retrieves it. Having got him to do that, leave him out of sight while you throw the object where he cannot see it. Then, using the same command, send him to look for it. By gradually increasing distance and length of time you leave the object, you should soon have a dog that can be taken to a certain spot and which will, on command, start searching. But he must never be cheated; always see that he finds something in the end. One day, if you drop a valuable wrist-watch by mistake in long grass, he will probably find it in a matter of minutes when it would take you hours and a great deal of luck to find it at all.

Useful variations of the retrieve are the 'seek back' and the 'seek forward', which are often the basis of tracking, whereby dogs not only find lost objects but lost people. This, of course, is a big subject, but you can amuse yourself and your dog without going into it very seriously.

To start the seek forward make the dog sit to heel, let him see that you have an object in your hand, then walk away from him, place the object out of sight instead of throwing it, and return on the same track. Of course, he knows roughly where you put the object and will go to look for it, but most dogs soon realize that all they have to do is follow your track to find the object at the end of it. You can then gradually increase the distance, and you can lay zig-zag tracks, but always walk back exactly on the same track.

Perhaps the best time to start teaching the seek back is when you are out for a walk. When the dog is running ahead free, surreptitiously drop a light object, such as a handkerchief, which he cannot hear fall. Proceed a few yards, call the dog back and send him to carry the object giving the usual command 'Carry'. Practise this until the dog will go back fifty yards or so for an object it can see. Having done that, start again in long grass and drop your handkerchief on or beside your track where the dog cannot see it. Begin by sending him a few yards and gradually increase the distance as with the seek forward.

In both exercises start with the command 'Carry' which the dog already knows, but soon precede it with another command, such as 'Seek', given in a slower, firmer tone. By going from 'Carry' to 'S-e-e-k carry', with all the emphasis on the

N

first word, the dog will soon learn the difference between tracking and retrieving. You can encourage this by pushing his head gently to the ground at the start of the track and indicating with the hand the direction in which you want him to seek. Practically any dog that is keen on retrieving can be taught to seek back or seek forward and many dogs, usually regarded as lap dogs, will go back a mile or more for an object dropped by their owner.

If you wish to go in for tracking seriously you should obtain more detailed instructions.[1] My reason for mentioning the subject here is because it can provide the average pet dog owner with an opportunity to develop one of the dog's instincts. A dog's greatest pleasures are derived from following its instincts, most of which, unfortunately, you will have to suppress in order to keep him out of trouble. Most dogs will derive as much pleasure from finding a 'lost' object as in chasing rabbits in the hedgerows, provided the latter has not become a habit. But, whereas the dog that chases rabbits is following an instinct as a means of amusing itself, the dog that retrieves is following the same instinct as a means of pleasing a master. The more you teach a dog the more it wants to be taught and the easier does it become to teach it. Instead, therefore, of the dog becoming an ever-increasing problem it becomes gradually more amenable and more attached to the owner who provides most of its pleasures. It can then, at any time, be taught any new exercise which the owner decides to teach it. Such a dog is not only a pleasure to own, it is a really useful animal and *far happier* and more contented than a dog that is forced to exist in luxurious idleness.

To end this book I should like to tell a story, an old one, that I remember well. When I left College and started working as Shepherd and Cattleman on my father's farm, he gave me a young Border Collie bitch called Floss.

Since I was a child I had taught dogs to do tricks, had used terriers as ratters, etc., and had worked dogs on both sheep and cattle, but I had never broken one from scratch. This one was, thanks to my father's attempts at breaking her, well behind scratch, for she had developed some very bad habits. However, a shepherd who gave me much valuable advice on both sheep

[1] These can be found in my book, *The Obedient Dog* (1975).

and sheepdogs assured me that she was a 'guid yin' and would be worth all the trouble. He also made some very unflattering remarks about the ability of my 'old man' and farmers in general to handle dogs, which I kept discreetly to myself!

About a year later another shepherd called. As it happened I wanted some cattle from a forty-acre field some distance from the 'steading' which stood on top of a hill. This field could be reached by a path through a wood, but the cattle had to be taken away to the far end of the field, where there was a gate on to the farm lane. As someone happened to be going out in the car, I asked him to open the gate and sent Floss for the cattle. While I busied myself with something else, she went, without further command, through the wood, gathered the cattle in the field, took them to the far end, through the gate, up the lane and put them all safely in the 'reed',[1] where she lay at the gate until I appeared; and where she would have stayed all night had I not appeared.

Unknown to me, this old shepherd had been watching all this and, when I went to shut the cattle in, he came up to me and said, 'That's a good bitch you've got there, lad.' To me, of course, he was only stating the obvious, and his remark merely added to the pride I already had.

I then pointed out that this was the first dog I had ever broken and asked if I had not made a good job of it. The reply was neither what I expected nor what I had hoped for. He looked straight at me and said in his soft Highland brogue: 'You know, when I was a lad my father gave me a dog, and I broke him myself, and he was a topper. I thought I had been very clever . . .' He paused, then went on: 'But that was nearly sixty years ago and I have bred the same strain ever since— that's one there,' pointing to the dog he had with him, 'but I've *never* had another like him.' I said nothing, but I never forgot those words. It is not yet sixty years since then, but it is over thirty—during which I have had more dogs through my hands than at that time I could have believed possible—but I have *never* had another like Floss. For a long time I thought and hoped that I might—I kept several of her daughters, but none was like her. Experience has taught me that I shall never have another Floss, because no two dogs are alike.

[1] yard 'Reed'=cattle.

Which brings us back to what I have been telling you all along. To have a good dog, for any purpose, the first essential is to get the right dog. The second is to understand that dog—not necessarily all dogs. If you are one of those lucky people who has a dog that never does anything wrong, that has only to be shown what to do to do it, I ask you to count your blessings.

Many people, like me in my inexperienced youth, regard themselves as clever trainers when they have merely been fortunate in getting an easily trained dog. Faced with a really difficult animal, many self-styled experts would look far more foolish than those they are ever anxious to ridicule.

Even if your dog is not a paragon, however, he may still be a wonderful friend to you. Don't forget that, to him, you should be not only a friend, but a master, almost a god, to whom he always looks up. It is up to you to make yourself worthy of such devotion. If you succeed you will be well repaid, but remember that you will never have another like him. *Never!*

CASTRATION AND SPAYING

HAVING had one Corgi castrated with nothing but beneficial effects we had first one then another of our own dogs castrated. At first I must admit that I almost expected to eventually regret doing something which could not be undone, but in no case did this happen. The question my wife and I now ask ourselves is not whether we should have a dog castrated but whether it is worth leaving him entire—just as horse breeders do and have always done with foals.

As a direct or indirect result of the many articles I have written on the subject I should think that hundreds of dogs have been castrated. Although I have had many letters expressing horror and disgust at the very thought of doing such a thing, all the letters from those who have done so have been full of gratitude. As people are so much more willing to write critical letters than praiseworthy ones I take this as a very good sign.

In spite of all that critics (mostly anthropomorphic theorists) have said on the subject I am quite convinced that under the circumstances which the average pet dog is kept a castrated dog is far happier than an entire one. 'It is cruel and wicked,' say my critics, 'to deprive him of one of his greatest pleasures in life.' A remark presumably based on their own ideas of pleasure! But circumstances have already removed this pleasure. How many pet dogs ever mate a bitch? And how many, in their efforts to do so, are pelted with buckets of water, old boots and even gunshot? This argument is like saying that it is kind to make a drunkard sit looking at a bottle of alcohol which he cannot reach but unkind to remove the bottle altogether! There is no truer saying than that what we don't want we don't miss.

This applies much more to a dog. Not being 'almost human' he does not grieve over what he might have done had someone not operated on him. Having started with one castrated dog among a lot of entire ones we have, at the time of writing, one entire dog and nine castrated ones. And I am convinced beyond a shadow of doubt that the 'geldings' are just as happy as the 'stallion' and some of them a good deal happier than they were before the operation. This is especially noticeable when bitches happen to be in season. While the entire dogs fret, howl and go off their food the others just do not worry at all.

So much for the advantages to the dog. What of the advantages to the owner? Since keeping gelded dogs of my own I have discovered far greater advantages than I first anticipated. All the unpleasant tendencies of the dog as opposed to the bitch are reduced if not removed entirely. Due to his having fewer other interests in life he is more amenable to training and more affectionate. He is less likely to fight and loses much of the entire dog's insatiable desire to go round leaving his 'visiting card' wherever he smells another dog— which often includes the furniture in someone else's house! And, of course, he is much less likely to go off on his own. Speaking generally I have found castrated dogs easier to handle and usually more pleasant animals to have around than entire ones. Here I might emphasize that I rarely have a dog castrated before a year (I shall explain why shortly) and, as I said earlier, I have had them operated on as late as six years old. Therefore apart from being able to compare castrated and entire dogs together I have also been able to compare the same dogs before and after operating.

One thing which became very apparent to me right from the start of my investigations was the difference between dogs castrated before and after maturity. Those neutered as puppies never seemed to develop. They lost their puppy charm without gaining any adult character. The guarding instinct never developed and many became over fat. In short they grew into great horrible 'eunuchs' which I had been assured was the inevitable result of castration in the dog. *But* I have never found a dog castrated as an adult to which any of this applied.

I feel certain that the chief reason for the long-standing prejudice against castrating dogs arises from the fact that so many have been neutered as puppies. Even today there are many veterinary surgeons who start off by warning their clients of the inadvisability of castrating a dog but, when the owner insists, will then say that the best age for carrying out the operation is between four and five months. From a purely surgical point of view all operations are easier on a young animal than on an older one. It is a lamentable fact that the veterinary profession as a whole, though so well versed in the physical ailments and well being of our animals, is still completely in the dark with regard to their mental development. Those who decry castration are condemning, not the operation, but their own stupidity in carrying it out when the animal is far too young.

The age at which dogs reach maturity varies considerably between individuals, small breeds usually maturing faster than larger ones. The first indication is usually when a dog starts lifting his leg and some people consider this the best age to operate. None of the male characteristics develop and he does not learn to lift his leg at all. The Guide Dogs for the Blind Association has trained quite a number of dogs castrated at this age. The majority have passed but others have failed to develop the initiative necessary in a guide dog. This, I believe, is due to their being castrated too young. But any dog which is likely to be easily distracted by lamp-posts, other dogs, etc., is useless for their purpose anyhow so they dare not risk leaving them too long. For my purpose, and I believe yours, it is better to leave a dog until all his male characteristics have fully developed, which may be any age from ten months to two years. Dogs castrated at this age do not entirely lose interest in the opposite sex (incidentally neither do horses) and we have several which have actually mated and tied with bitches in season. But only when they have nothing better to do and the bitch is 'bang on'! We exercise and work our bitches in season with gelding dogs without any of them ever bothering. And they pay far less attention to strange dogs which we meet when working on location. Otherwise they retain the masculine appearance and character which I like to see in any male animal, gelded or otherwise.

In spite of the improvement it leads to in the average dog, castration should not be regarded as a magic cure for all evils. As an aid to training it is sometimes invaluable but it is never a substitute. Nor is it a cure for bad temperament. I have met owners who have had their dog castrated on the advice of their veterinary surgeon because it had a tendency to bite members of the family. As no improvement had resulted they have come to me for advice. And the first thing I discover is that the dog is a shy biter—he bites through fear, not aggressiveness. No one with even a rudimentary understanding of the canine mind would expect this type of temperament to be improved by castration. An over-aggressive dog with a strong pack-leader instinct will probably be improved but the instinct of fear has no connection with the instinct of sex and it is only those characteristics associated with this instinct which are changed by castration.

The same applies to fighting dogs. As I said earlier on, fighters can be divided roughly into three groups. Those which fight for fun, those which fight because of the guarding instinct and those which fight through fear. Directly or indirectly it is the pack-leading instinct which creates the desire to fight in the first two categories. In both cases castration will considerably reduce the aggressive tendencies although it is not a miracle cure for a dog that has become an habitual fighter. The dog which fights through fear is an entirely different proposition and I have found nothing which has any effect at all.

My own first-hand experience of spayed bitches is not so extensive as that of castrated dogs. I have, however, gathered a great deal of information from the Guide Dogs for the Blind Association where bitches are used almost exclusively. Some years ago a representative went to the U.S.A. where spaying of bitches is universal in Guide Dogs and general in pet dogs. Since then it has become general practice to spay all bitches intended for training. I have had many discussions on this subject with the experts concerned and, being a frequent visitor to the Guide Dog Training Centre at Leamington, have seen a great many spayed bitches.

The most important facts emerging from the research into this subject are (1) bitches spayed before they have come into season show a marked tendency to glandular troubles and obesity and (2) bitches spayed after having been in season once do not change at all.

The chief benefit to the bitch is that she will not have to be shut up for three weeks every six months. Or worse still be allowed to mate and have the resultant unwanted puppies destroyed at birth. The other advantage is that she will not develop uterine troubles so common later in life. Our Border Collie Tuck, well known for her part as 'Clive' in the B.B.C. series *Cluff*, started developing irregular and abnormal seasons. At eight she was spayed and lived to be thirteen fitter, healthier and 'younger' than she had been for years before.

Bitches which are subject to false pregnancies must suffer considerably and this problem, too, can be solved with spaying. The great advantage to the owner is that it saves the trouble of coping with a bitch in season. To some (blind people for instance) this is a very real advantage. To others it is simply an aid to laziness. Unlike castration, which can be carried out under a local anaesthetic, spaying is a major operation requiring a good deal of after care until the wound heals. For these reasons we give much more thought to spaying than we do to castration. But our spayed bitches have never shown any ill effects. Here I might add that we have always had the services of some of the most skilled veterinary surgeons in the country, especially in surgery.

The advantages of neutering dogs and bitches do not end with the animals and their owners. If the practice became general—and it is becoming increasingly common—the advantage to this country as a whole would be inestimable. In my introduction I refer to the appalling amount of dog trouble to which Britain is prone, a state of affairs which has become worse in recent years. There can be no doubt that this is due largely to the modern craze for so-called dog sanctuaries where stray and unwanted dogs are kept, sometimes under appalling conditions, until they are found new homes. What people overlook is that the reason many of these dogs are unwanted is because they are thoroughly unlikeable creatures. Bred from a line of vagrants and delinquents their ancestry and upbringing renders them quite unsuitable as family pets. A fact which many a kind-hearted dog lover has soon discovered on taking one into his or her home. The result is that many escape to enjoy life and cause trouble until they are run over, foisted on to some other unsuspecting dog lover or find themselves back in a sanctuary

—in other words, back in prison. The R.S.P.C.A. estimates that British animal welfare societies deal with some 300,000 unwanted dogs *every year* nearly all young healthy animals. All of which points to one inescapable fact—Great Britain is overrun with dogs. Anything which will reduce the number will benefit dogs, dog owners and the general public. An increase in the licence fee so often advocated cannot have any effect for the simple reason that a stray dog rarely has an owner let alone a licence. And those which do have owners rarely have licences either!

It must be obvious to anyone that a general policy of neutering pet dogs and bitches would automatically reduce the dog population. What may not be so obvious is that the effect would be mainly on the type of dog which causes most trouble —the dog bred to roam which has no desire to live as a contented family dog.

In recent years the practice of neutering cats, both male and female, has increased considerably. As a result one sees fewer cats. More important, one sees fewer half-starved, mangy, unwanted cats. I believe that a similar practice would have the same effect on the dog population. The only people who could fail to gain from such a policy would be those who have established sanctuaries and would have no stray dogs to imprison.

Veterinary surgeons are now less reluctant to neuter dogs or bitches and some even advocate it. My own vet, who is also a successful breeder and trainer of dogs, agrees wholeheartedly with my views on the subject. But I still meet dogs castrated as puppies and bitches spayed before they have been in season; all too often with obvious undesirable results. One can only hope that one day the veterinary profession which does so much for the dog's physical wellbeing will take more interest in the conditions which affect its mentality.

Some animal welfare societies, at one time loud in their condemnation of castration or spaying, now actually recommend it. But while anxious to single out the individual with whom they disagree any good ideas always come from themselves! They talk of sterilization as if it was some new idea they had discovered, whereas I first wrote about it some twenty years ago. But that is only human nature and what really matters is that there is an increasing tendency to neuter dogs and bitches and this can have nothing but beneficial results.

One of those results is that the once big problem of whether to have a dog or a bitch is now hardly a problem at all. All the objections to having a dog can be removed to a greater or lesser degree by castration and the one objection to a bitch (that she comes in season) can be removed entirely by spaying. One can therefore allow characteristics like size and appearance to influence one's decision on whether to have a dog or a bitch. Dogs are usually bigger than bitches, more so in some breeds than others. In natural breeds, bred exclusively for work, one finds a big variation in size. A notable example is the Husky where the dogs often weigh nearly twice as much as the bitches and it is also apparent in breeds like the working collie and gundogs. But in most of the toy breeds one finds dogs smaller than the bitches. This is entirely unnatural and can have nothing but harmful results.

Many of these little dogs are effeminate and 'cissy'. When I am choosing a dog I like to know that he is a dog when he is standing facing me. Even when I am choosing a puppy from a litter I like to be able to sort the dogs from the bitches without turning them over. But if I like the look of what I believe to be a bitch puppy and on examination find it to be a dog I would not have it at any price. If on the other hand, I fancy a dog and find that it is a bitch I should have no objection at all. Many of our best bitches have been decidedly masculine in appearance and their sexual behaviour has been somewhat peculiar to say the least of it! These 'doggy' bitches have, however, been excellent workers and companions and, although I don't favour this type as a brood bitch, some of them have bred quite well. But I have yet to meet a 'bitchy' dog that was worth the food he ate. Whether you intend having him castrated or keeping him entire it is most important to choose a dog that really *is* a dog.

INDEX